THE
AMAZON
Self
PUBLISHER

HOW TO SELL MORE BOOKS ON AMAZON

DALE L. ROBERTS

FOREWORD BY JULIE BROAD

The Amazon Self Publisher: How to Sell More Books on Amazon is a series of books including:

Amazon Keywords for Books: How to Use Keywords for Better Discovery on Amazon

Original publication date: September 15, 2020

Promotional Strategies for Books: How to Market & Promote Your Book

Original publication date: October 1, 2020

Amazon Reviews for Books: How to Get Book Reviews on Amazon

Original publication date: November 1, 2020

By Dale L. Roberts

©2020 One Jacked Monkey, LLC

Some recommended links in this book are part of affiliate programs. This means if you purchase a product through one of the links, then I get a portion of each sale. It doesn't affect your cost and greatly helps support the cause. If you have any reservations about buying a product through my affiliate link, then feel free to Google a direct link and bypass the affiliate link.

Cover design by a Fiverr seller. To see the full process of how we created the cover design, watch the video at https://dalelinks.com/5designs.

Cover design by MaMarko78 on Fiverr. To see his services, visit https://dalelinks.com/coversbymarko.

Find out how I found Marko and why I selected him for cover design services in the video at https://dalelinks.com/5designs.

Interior formatting by Archangel Ink at DaleLinks.com/ArchangelInk.

ISBN: 978-1-950043-25-5

Are you ready to begin your own self-publishing journey?
You have a story.
It deserves to be told.

Learn the fundamentals of self-publishing books…

In this in-depth, yet succinct, course.

The DIY Publishing Course for Beginners

It's perfect for anyone new to the self-publishing business!
It will take you from manuscript to self-published.

The best part? It's 100% free!

Visit DIYPublishing.biz/Free to enroll today.

o you ever go to your favorite web browser and ask it questions? I'm constantly searching for things like "how are rocks formed?" and "how can I make a snow globe?" because I'm the mom of an intelligent, curious boy who asks me questions that are beyond my expertise. I'm a fan of getting help online, but if you are asking search engines to help you figure out how to write, publish, and promote a book, do so with caution. When you do a search, for example, on "how to run Amazon Ads for books," you'll uncover all of the following: bad advice, regurgitated bad advice, generic advice, and good advice. How do you figure out which advice falls into what category?

It can even be confusing and overwhelming for *me*, and I'm an Amazon overall #1 bestselling author (yes, number one in the category of Books on Amazon). I'm also in the business of helping people write, publish, and promote non-fiction books. My company, Book Launchers, and my YouTube channel, BookLaunchers.TV, provide a ton of support, services, and sound advice for helping authors succeed in publishing. So, if I find it hard to wade through all the online advice for selling a book on Amazon, I can only imagine how it feels when you're a new author and a novice book marketer.

Luckily… you've picked up the book that is going to change all that.

Dale is a fitness author turned self-publishing expert and for years he's been my go-to resource for so many of my questions about keywords, promotional strategies, Amazon ads, and the latest in Amazon updates. He's on the platform every single day, testing, learning, and then teaching strategies on YouTube for his rapidly growing audience at Self-Publishing with Dale. He finally took all of that years of accumulated expertise and packaged it up into one perfect resource to help authors of fiction and non-fiction books market their books effectively on Amazon—without blowing a budget or following bad advice (Amazon Bestseller Gimmicks anyone?!).

You should pay special attention to the juicy tips he shares on Amazon relevancy and the underused tools Amazon gives you to market your book. I must confess, I immediately took a few of the ones we weren't using at Book Launchers and applied them to the books we're working on with our clients. Thanks, Dale! You're also going to cut through all the noise when it comes to understanding what's crucial for promoting your book, as well as how to gather the oh-so-important and also challenging-to-get Amazon reviews. In other words: you're set up for Amazon success after you read this.

So, what you really need to do is read this book right now. I only have two things left to say. The first is, you are *in* good hands... actually, you are holding in your hands a book written by one of the smartest and most generous folks I've met since getting into the publishing industry. You have chosen well. The second: remember that the greatest gift you can give any author is a review. After you read and love this book (because I know you will!) please write Dale a killer review on Amazon because... Well, karma! You're going to need a lot of reviews so it's only fair you write some too, right?

I wish you much success,

Julie, the "Book Broad."

Amazon Overall #1 Bestselling Author and Founder of Book Launchers

Self Publisher ▾ **Contents** 🔍

AMAZON KEYWORDS *for* BOOKS

HOW TO USE KEYWORDS FOR BETTER DISCOVERY ON AMAZON

| Keywords ▾ | **Contents** | 🔍 |

Contents

Walking into the crowded hotel lobby, I scanned the clusters of people for a familiar face. That situation was already overwhelming, but now imagine my usually introverted mind reeling at the prospect of starting a conversation with a complete stranger. But, that wouldn't have to happen if only I found one person I knew. And, bingo! There he was, Dan Norton. Now, rather than go into the gory details of who Dan is or how we know each other, I'll just say he and I share quite a few mutual loves. One of our shared interests is pro wrestling.

Naturally, as I'm walking up to Dan, I see he's talking to a mutual acquaintance, Andru Edwards. Oddly enough, Andru and I have crossed paths many times, and each time we share a common love – pro wrestling. See where this is going yet? Andru and I are both former pro wrestlers. He'd trained on the east coast, whereas I trained in Calgary, Alberta, Canada. But, it's that bond the two of us share that makes for easy conversation and ways for us to catch up with each other.

At a previous conference where we'd run into each other, I discovered he was trained by one of my all-time favorites. So, when I approached the two, I was elated to discover they were talking about our shared love – pro wrestling. I promise this is going somewhere, just stay with me.

"Hey, Dan, did you know that Andru is a trained pro wrestler?" I asked.

"No, I didn't," Dan responded.

The three of us chatted like excited children. We'd shared favorite matches, favorite wrestlers, locker room etiquette, and the whole she-bang. Now and then, folks would wander by us and tune in to our conversation. Another fellow video creator, Mike Vardy, popped into the conversation at one point to share he had a tattoo tribute to his favorite wrestler.

And, though people would briefly visit our small group of wrestling enthusiasts, the four of us stayed. Some people would come to listen in and chime in their favorite parts of the sport. Others would hear a bit about what we were talking about and just move on.

The shared interest and theme of the conversation was pro wrestling. Now, this book isn't so much about pro wrestling at all. In fact, that'll probably be the last you hear of it. It's more about the concept of a conversation or shared interest. That's where keywords lie. I'd imagine had we all not had that shared interest, this would be a bit more stilted and hard to convey. But, we shared this love for pro wrestling, a pre-determined sport that has a niche audience. We would've been limited to the two or three of us had no one had an interest. But, we had a few people who were very much interested or mildly intrigued by what we were talking about.

When people tuned into the conversation, they heard the general theme and the specific word or derivative of "wrestle." That's what kept people coming. And, that's how keywords function in the online ethos. A keyword is a beacon shining from the lighthouse guiding ships away from rocky terrain and onto safer shores. Keywords are the shared interests people have and the way for people to identify with other people. Without keywords, online users would be forced to mindlessly scroll through websites, trying to find what they're looking for.

Sure, every blind squirrel gets a nut. However, without keywords, we'd be lost and forced to figure things out on our own. With keywords, you significantly increase your likelihood of finding precisely what you're looking for.

That's what we did in that crowded lobby that night. The three of us had a shared interest. We spoke about what we loved. We didn't have to think about "profitable" ways to express ourselves, or what was the best way to call a wrestling move. We just talked about it. When people gathered around us, they knew what the conversation was about and if it was of any interest to them.

As you go through this book, you're going to discover more basic concepts that'll help you see an overview of the business of keywords. We'll also dive deeper into more advanced concepts. Even if you were to put this book down now, I'm confident if you follow this advice you'll get pretty far:

> Describe your book in a few words. Don't worry about profitability. Don't worry about trying to gather an audience. Don't worry about saying the right thing or the wrong thing. Just say it. The rest will fall into place.

I know many would-be experts will be quick to correct me. These are the same folks who feel you shouldn't follow your passion. They'd rather have you grind it out and hope for the best. However, I'm going to be real with you. You aren't writing and publishing books for a machine. You're writing and publishing books for people. Real people. Once you get past the whole part of trying to game the system or trick Amazon into doing your bidding, you'll discover that *people* buy books. Algorithms and search engines don't buy books.

But, if you want to increase your odds for success, it's sometimes best to know what to say, how to say it, when you should say it, and where you should say it. That way, you open your circle of influence and welcome more like-minded people. That's what it's about. Grow your circle of friends. Welcome more people into the conversation. And, nurture those relationships. That's when you'll see your audience grow exponentially as the days, weeks, months, and years go on.

I encourage you to read on and take notes as you go. You may have to go back and reread some sections. Lord knows it took me over 6 years to even get this basic understanding of how keywords function on the Amazon marketplace. I don't imagine a short book will get you the same knowledge as I have, but I'll point you in the right direction. By the end of this book, you'll have all the information to select the ideal keywords for publishing your books on Amazon by way of Kindle Direct Publishing. Read on!

What Are Keywords?

Keywords are the bridge connecting a customer to a potential outcome or product. When you want to learn more about something, you open a browser, type into the search window what you believe you want to find, and the search engine scrapes online options for the best fit. Deeper insights reveal more complexity when it comes to how a search engine finds what it does. For now, just know a keyword is how a customer tries to find something.

Many people misunderstand keywords and view them like a game of *Buzzword* or *Taboo*. The misconception is a keyword only consists of a single word. But, that's the furthest from the truth. In fact, a keyword can be one or more words forming a phrase. Heck, some of the best keywords are phrases that are a string of 3 or more words. Why are they the best? Because it narrows down the search and dramatically increases the odds of a customer finding what they're looking for.

For instance, I might look for ways to exercise. But, I have a litany of injuries and limitations, so not all exercises are going to suit me. If I simply used the keyword "exercise" to search options, I may get a ton of popular exercise options that are unsuitable for me. However, if I target my search a bit more, then my search results will bring back items a bit more appropriate for me. What if I use "back injury exercises" or "exercises to strengthen the back"? Now, I've narrowed down the search to something a lot more appropriate to what I want and need.

We could dive even deeper into our search and get more granular by getting even more specific. Maybe I could search "30-day exercise program to strengthen the back." Wow! Now, I've gotten time-specific in my targeting. And, I've eliminated a whole lot. Can you imagine the results had I just chosen "exercise" as my search query?

If I used "exercise" as my only descriptor to find what I need, I'd be searching for hours to find what would best fit me. But, once I got specific about what I needed, the search engine has more to work with and can narrow down the options.

Try it out for yourself. Go to Amazon and type in the word "exercise." How many results came back? How many of those results interest you or are even suitable for your needs?

Now, get more specific about the type of exercise you want. Get *really* granular in your search. Choose something time-specific, age-based, and goal-based. See what the search results bring back. Most likely, you're going to find more suitable options for your needs.

And, that's how keywords work. They aren't just a single term people use to find what they're looking for. The best keywords are phrases or a string of words that pull up something specific to your wants and needs.

Why Are Keywords Important?

You'd think I hammered the point home with the previous section, but now we have to look at it from a content creator's standpoint. As a writer or publisher, we're always looking for ways to get more sales. Naturally, our minds gravitate towards the best keywords to draw in the most potential customers, but we forget about the human experience in the process. When you try to publish books for an algorithm or search engine, you lose sight of the original point – to sell more books to *people*.

We want to connect with more readers, not search queries. That's why you need to get good on who your audience is.

Identify Your Ideal Reader

Before even putting pen to paper, you should identify your ideal reader. This is the person you want to read your book. No, you should not be writing a book for everyone. Because when you try to please everyone, you'll please no one in the process.

About 6 years ago, when I published my first book, I was quick to share it with anyone and everyone. One of those people was a friend and marketing expert, Mark Stafford. We sat down for a casual lunch when I stuffed my published book into his hands.

The first question Mark asked was, "Who is your target audience?"

"Everyone," I said.

Mark narrowed his vision on the cover, leafed through the book, and appeared to ponder on the best response.

"Everyone? This can't be for everyone. Who do you see buying this book?" he asked.

"Everyone. I made an exercise book good for everyone from kids to senior citizens," I said.

"That's not possible. Senior citizens can't work out the same as kids would. Did you give advice for both in different chapters?"

He stumped me. I really thought my book was meant for everyone. In my mind, it was at the time. But, when I thought about it, I'd never gotten good on who I was writing for. My first book was hammered garbage to put it nicely.

Rather than take Mark's advice to heart, I spent the better part of two years struggling to make ends meet as a full-time author. Why? Because I didn't get good on who my audience was.

Once you identify your ideal reader or your target audience, the rest becomes easier. Much like defining your purpose:

> When you identify your why, the how becomes easy.

When I finally identified my ideal reader, I could then begin to figure out why they'd look for my book. Once I figured out my ideal reader's purpose, I then theorized ways they would search for my book. That's what you want to do.

1. Who is your reader?

2. Why are they looking for your book?

3. What is your ideal reader's pain point?

4. How would they look for your book?

Once you answer those four questions, you can then list several keywords as potential candidates. These keywords act as bridges to your products or different avenues leading to your book.

What Are the Different Types of Keywords?

Now comes the nerdy stuff. You don't need to remember the terms and don't worry if you don't get the nuances right away. But, it's a good idea to get a look under the hood, so you know how and why keywords function the way they do. We'll revisit these throughout this book.

The single term keyword phrase is commonly known as the root keyword. In our previous example of "exercise," that was our root keyword. The root signifies the base of the topic. We can all agree exercise takes many forms, so that's why it's the root keyword.

Now, think about other root keywords besides exercise. Here are a few:

- Romance

- Science Fiction

- Politics

- Christianity

Do you see how simple that was? Did you notice what I did in the previous list? There's one keyword that should stick out like a sore thumb. Look back. Do you see it?

"Science Fiction" is the one root keyword with two words in it. How is this a root keyword, then?

Root keywords don't always have to be a single term. They can consist of multiple words. The root keyword is a general category search. As you can imagine, "science fiction" takes many forms, including:

- Science fiction romance

- Military science fiction

- Post-apocalyptic science fiction

- Space opera science fiction

- Werebear shapeshifter romance science fiction

Okay, okay. The last one might be a stretch, but it's more to prove a point that a root keyword is merely a jumping-off point and not so much a single term alone. A root keyword is the most generalized way of identifying a customer's search. It's the other words in the keyword phrase that act as descriptors.

The next type of keyword is a long-tail keyword. As you can imagine, this is a full keyword phrase made up of about three or more words strung together. Long-tail keywords are the most granular approach to searching online. When we built out a search for my exercise needs, we got very specific on time, goals, and special needs. The full phrase represented a long-tail keyword search term.

You won't often hear me say long-tail keyword in the book or on video. Why? Because it's easier for me to say keyword. Could I be more specific? Yes, because then I'd be more precise with my audience. Do you see the mistake I made? I illustrate the importance of using a root keyword versus a long-tail keyword. Rather than using the root keyword of "keyword" alone, I could be more specific. Once I'm more specific, my audience gets a better understanding of what's going on. Pretty cool, right?

That's how long-tail keywords work. When you get specific, your audience gets a better understanding.

Often, I hear would-be experts and self-professed gurus who say self-publishing is saturated. That's furthest from the truth. The fact is many people have tapped into all the root keywords for easy search volume. Now, we're faced with getting more granular with our audience and identifying the many ways customers search for a solution to their problems. The market isn't saturated. Plenty of consumers are still looking for solutions to their problems. You just have to figure out how they're searching.

And, the best part is the consuming audience always changes the way they use search engines. Dialects change, popular trends change, and descriptors change. The market is ever-changing. All you have to do is identify where an opportunity exists and deliver the goods when someone finds your content.

How Can You Search Different Types of Keywords?

Here's where we'll get into the nitty-gritty of keywords because now we'll discuss keyword types. These keyword types are used most commonly in ad campaigns through services like Google Ads, Facebook Ads, and something we'll cover later, Amazon Ads. Knowing the various keyword types will help you refine your approach and possibly leverage the power of online advertising.

Once you get a fundamental understanding of advertising online, you'll be able to pay for data that'll serve you up the exact audience you want. The audience reveals itself through what they're searching to discover your book and if they buy your book based on that search.

If a customer isn't buying, then most likely, there's a disconnect. Now, rather than going into how the book cover and book description play a vital role in the conversion of the sale, we'll simply focus on the keyword that gets them there. What we'll get into later, ultimately, is that the keyword can drive traffic to your book. But, if it doesn't convert into a sale, it may not be the issue with the keyword, especially if it has perceived relevance.

The first type of keyword is a broad match. A broad match keyword is when you have a general search of a keyword that can be configured any way you make it, shake it, or bake it. When using a broad keyword match, you could use a simple keyword like "exercise at home." The search engine is going to play word jumble and selective use with those words.

For instance, a broad keyword match for "exercise at home" could get search volume for:

- Home exercise

- No exercise

- At home recipes

- Home cooking

- Home buying

- Group exercise

Do you see how vague a broad keyword match is? It's like telling the advertising platform to serve up just about anyone. Can you imagine the context of the original conversation about "wrestling?" It would be like if someone came up who was an amateur stand-out and heard us talking about wrestling only to discover it's the sports entertainment variety and not the Olympic-style wrestling.

Broad keyword matches are suitable for advertising campaigns for cheaper clicks. But, with cheaper clicks, you get a larger audience who doesn't want your book. That's okay because you're casting a wide net, identifying the quick victories and low-hanging fruit.

Think of broad keyword matches like this:

> Wide net = wide audience + low relevance

The next type of keyword is a broad modifier. These types of keywords are when you're looking for deviations of your broad keyword. Let's go back to our original keyword example, "exercise at home." But, this time in an advertising campaign, we'll use the "+" symbol before a word to identify our need for deviation. You'd place the plus symbol before the word you wish to have a bit more flexibility. This allows for a broader search while getting a bit more granular search results. Rather than limiting it to a specific type of word, we can then use it in many ways.

In this instance, we'd use "+exercise +at +home."

- Exercising at home
- Homesteading
- Homeschooling exercises
- Exercises at the fitness institute
- At the Drive-In

Do you see how the results bring back a crazy list of very different results? But, your chances as an advertiser to identify an audience have significantly increased, especially if you see conversions. And, the best part is it unearths possibilities you'd never thought about. With these new possibilities, you may open yourself to a potential audience you never knew had an interest in your book.

Think of broad modified keywords like this:

Wide net with flexibility =
wide audience + more granular

Try this fun little test out. Go to Google and type in "+exercise +at +home" and see what results you get. I'm sure it'll be way different than my random examples above. Take note of all the possibilities and pay the closest attention to the bolded words in each search result. That represents the broad modified match.

The broad modified keyword presents more flexible search results like this example.

The next two keyword types are the holy grails of keywords. Once you get these keywords dialed in, you'll most likely have killer ad campaigns and a book with crazy organic traffic. This means you'll be getting a high return on investment for your ads, and people will find your book easily with the keywords you've selected.

The first of the two holy grail keyword types is exact match. An exact match is when a customer uses a keyword, and your book gets served based on exactly matching your keyword. Ultimately, if you're running any ad campaigns, you'll want to leverage the power of broad and broad modified keywords. Then, identify exact keywords that lead to the sale of your book. Those exact keywords are the exact matches you'll use in future ad campaigns because they were successful in turning a browsing customer into a buyer.

It's the exact match keyword that will often be the best selection for your book's information. Will you be able to rely on an exact match forever? Most likely not, but you'll soon discover the power of relevancy and the shelf-life of a keyword.

Often, an exact match is represented by quotes around the keyword. Try this out for yourself. Go to Google and search for "exercises at home" but include the quotes this time. What you're doing is telling the search engine you want only *exercises at home* and no deviation of that.

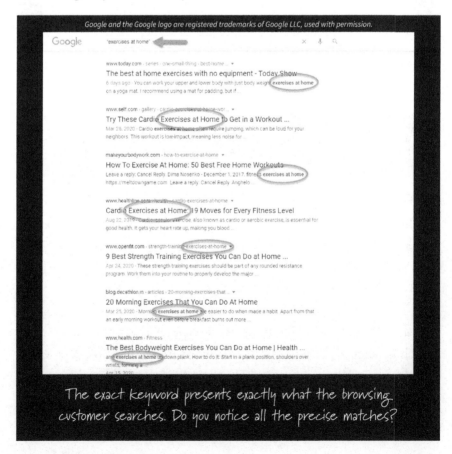

The exact keyword presents exactly what the browsing customer searches. Do you notice all the precise matches?

The help page for Kindle Direct Publishing even discourages publishers from using quotes in their seven keyword slots (covered later in the book). Why? Because it dramatically inhibits the number of searches since you're not allowing for any wiggle room. I'll agree wholeheartedly on that point. You can use exact matches in an ad campaign, and in most instances, you won't have to use the quotes. However, avoid using the quotes in your book's information, because you diminish the ability to reach more readers and search queries.

As you build out and scale up your ad campaigns, you ultimately want to have exact match keyword campaigns. But you also want to build up an ad campaign with the next keyword variation, the phrase match.

The phrase match works along with exact matches the same way a broad modified keyword works with broad keywords, but a keyword phrase match is asking for the exact keyword with some variation or deviation. This way, it opens your campaign's or book's likelihood of discovery to more audiences. It will also reveal other possibilities that'll work in your favor.

When it comes to exact match and phrase match, remember this:

> Exact Match = Smallest net = exact audience + higher relevance + hyper-targeted audience
>
> Phrase match = Exact keyword with variation = smaller net + higher relevance + targeted audience

As you read on, you might find this section a bit muddy since it's merely laying the groundwork. Get at least a basic understanding of these concepts. Then, you can better grasp the more advanced concepts as we move along. Do you need to run ad campaigns to be successful? No, but do you increase your odds of success using paid advertising? Possibly. As long as you know what you're doing. At the end of the book, you'll get some of my trusted resources and reliable experts in advertising.

How Does a Search Engine Work?

Oddly enough, a lot of how keywords work is through the power of the search engine. But, the search engine is simply what the audience sees as a website with a box where you type up something you want to find online. Even so, it's far more complicated than you'd think. No, there's no magical gnomes who read your mind and serve you the precise thing you want. And, no, it's not as simple as the search engine guessing what a browsing consumer wants.

Search engines function on algorithms, a complex mathematical formula. After years of billions of search queries, Google has algorithmic programming down to a science. And, the Google algorithm becomes more complex and sophisticated with every passing day and every single search.

In layman's terms, an algorithm is a formula that tries to predict user behavior based on past user behaviors and related behaviors of similar audiences. For instance, when a browsing customer searches for "home-cooked recipes for weight loss," the search engine gets to work in a few ways. It figures out what's the best fit for the customer based on previous search history, past consuming habits, and other people who share the same types of behaviors. Crazy, right?

A search engine serves results to a browsing consumer based on relevance. For the sake of less confusion, I'm going to separate two types of relevance. When I refer to relevance by itself, then I mean algorithmic relevance. The second type is perceived relevance or what we believe to be relevant to a book or search query.

Algorithmic relevance is based on a formula and a potentially positive outcome. When a consumer searches for something and they don't find it, then the algorithm will determine the results weren't relevant to the consumer. However, when a consumer searches and clicks to view more content or even buys an item, the algorithm adjusts. It will then deem the search result with a positive outcome as relevant to the search term.

On Amazon, if a customer searches for "nursery rhymes for babies," the algorithm is going to view past behaviors based on this search term. It's going to review the products with the best results and conversions – be it sales or views – and serve the customer several product suggestions. But wait, it gets a little more complicated. The Amazon algorithm is going to account for previous search history, buying behavior, and other similar customer search history and buying behaviors. Then, the Amazon algorithm serves up the products it theorizes to be the most relevant to that customer.

This is what a lot of would-be experts in self-publishing get wrong time and again. They elude to finding the magical keyword or keyword phrase methodology. And, they'll even share some best practices for finding a keyword the purest way possible. But, what they fail to realize is the algorithm isn't a one-size-fits-all formula. It's more customized to each browsing customer's needs. Based on what that customer does next, the algorithm adjusts accordingly.

If you ever want to test it out, I recommend you search for any random item on Amazon. Choose something you'd never buy. Click on the product, read the full description, and then scroll down and choose additional products related to it. Spend about 20 to 30 minutes doing this. In fact, add a few of the items to your shopping cart (don't worry, you don't have to buy them).

Now, take a break from Amazon for a day or two. Then, come back to Amazon on its home page and discover all the items it'll serve you. It'll be a weird mixture of what you usually like and then this random item you'd never buy.

It's kind of like going onto a used car lot and telling the salesman you're interested in a Mercedes Benz, and you want to see all the models. The used car salesman might be confused because he clearly saw you rolling into the parking lot in your beat-up 1997 Ford Ranger. But, he's gonna go with it. Then, after you're done shopping, you leave and come back and tell him you're interested in buying a truck. That used car salesman is going to be so confused because he thought you wanted something a bit more luxury-related. But, he's still not surprised you want to look at trucks since that's what you originally arrived in.

The Amazon algorithm is a fickle beast, and anyone who tells you they know precisely how it acts is a little full of themselves or something else altogether. The Amazon algorithm bases its actions on consumer actions and reactions, then adjusts from there.

And, that's where reality versus perception comes into play. Where we think we know the answer, the algorithm has more in-depth insights than we can even begin to fathom. So, while we can theorize a keyword set will bring success to a book, the algorithm will ultimately decide if the customers genuinely want it. And, if you're a new author who has published your first book, you're working on rolling a boulder uphill.

The fewer books you have as an author, the fewer opportunities you have to gain the favor of the Amazon algorithm.

Are Search Engine Algorithms the Same Across Platforms?

Are search engine algorithms the same across all platforms? Is the Google search engine algorithm the same as the Amazon algorithm? Or, is the Facebook algorithm the same as the Amazon algorithm? Though the principles are somewhat the same, the audience is different. After all, the audience might be different ages and from different regions. The audience might have different languages or different dialects. Each audience has a different belief system and different needs. And, the most critical part is the actual audience size per platform and the amount of time the search engine has been used.

Google, by far, is the most sophisticated of all search engines. Why is that? It's because it is the most popular and most widely used search engine in the world. The more customers use Google, the more the algorithm begins to refine its search results. And, the more repeat customers Google has, the more the algorithm can predictively serve results that most match a customer's wants and needs.

Google has been getting billions of searches since its inception, so it has a leg up on all search engines across every platform. So, where does that leave Amazon? A few years ago, I read an article stating that Amazon's search engine is about 5 years behind Google's. The reason? Though Amazon is the online retail juggernaut, its online traffic pales in comparison to what Google has.

That doesn't mean Amazon's algorithm is archaic by any stretch. It's still rather sophisticated, but think of Amazon's algorithm like the little brother to the Google algorithm. Since Google dominates search traffic, it behooves every business using a search engine algorithm to take notes and implement what they're doing. That equates to more repeat customers and, most importantly, happy customers. After all, if you can get more people what they want out of life, then you can get everything you want too. That's how search engines function – to deliver the best results possible to the consumer.

As the world shifted in early 2020 to social distancing, now more than ever, online sales and traffic are a necessity. That means more consumer traffic will help to refine search engine algorithms. Amazon will start to pick up steam since customers who used to be steadfast about ordering products in a store are now forced to buy from the online retailer.

If you look at social media platforms, you'll discover quite a few functions on a search engine. Facebook, for example, has a search engine algorithm. And, quite a bit of it is about discovering what their users want most so they can deliver the goods. Then, Facebook leverages that information for online advertising dollars. Is Facebook's algorithm as sophisticated as Google or Amazon? Not by any stretch. But again, it has the same fundamental principles as both those search engine algorithms do.

Even if you were to quit reading this book right now, I'd implore if you want to master the art of keywords, then study search engine algorithms. Then apply what you know about your ideal audience, and you've got a winning formula. How do you begin to understand relevance? Also, how do you build algorithmic relevance for your book?

How Do You Build Relevance for a Keyword?

How exactly do you get a book to be relevant for a given keyword? In theory, if you find a keyword with high search volume and low competition or use, then you should be able to win, right? Not really. I've tested that theory dozens of times. And, though a few might catch lightning in a bottle, the vast majority of authors and publishers don't. Why is that? It has a lot to do with getting your chance to shine and dropping the ball.

For the record, Amazon loves new products. In fact, they love new products so much, Amazon even created a special category for new publications called New Releases. This works for both fiction and nonfiction and in print books and ebooks. The first thirty days of publishing a book are magical on Amazon. Once you publish your book, the clock starts ticking. If you cannot prove to be a winning commodity, you'll be buried in the search traffic after the first month.

Amazon's Hot New Releases list showcases all the best performing books in a category from the past 30 days.

At the end of the day, the place every author covets is the first-page search results. Why? Because let's face it, not many consumers make it past the first page. Some will hardly scroll down the page to see the full results. Creator of Publisher Rocket and Kindlepreneur.com, Dave Chesson, said the highest converting spot to be was in the first position of the first-page search results. After that, your odds of converting a sale diminish the further down your book is in search results. Then, oddly enough, your odds increase at the last spot of the first-page search.[1]

Is it as simple as adding a keyword to your book's information? Can you simply identify a profitable keyword, put it in your book info, and get the first-page placement? Not really. Remember, the search engine algorithm customizes search results to each customer based on their browsing history and buying patterns.

So, what builds algorithmic relevance? Quite a few items help in building relevance for your title. Of course, the king of all metrics is the sale. If you can get a sale, then you've got a chance. But, that doesn't explain how some titles start winning right after publishing with no advertising and no real audience. Enter impressions.

As mentioned before, Amazon loves new products and wants to give any new product a shot. So, it'll start to serve a book to an audience based on the keywords used and the categories selected for a book. When a customer searches for a book on Amazon and Amazon serves the results, that's when an impression occurs. Once Amazon presents a product to a customer, it's known as an impression.

> Fun fact: In Amazon Advertising, impressions are free. This is a further reason to use Amazon Advertising to build relevance for your book.

The next most crucial action comes when the customer makes a decision. Does the customer continue to scroll and look at the next page of results? If so, then the recommended products proved to have less relevance to that customer. That doesn't mean Amazon won't serve those results again. But, it does mean that based on the customer's browsing behavior and buy patterns, Amazon is less likely to serve those products again.

So, in some instances, an unheard-of book gets it's one time to shine through a search query. If a browsing customer passes the chance to view more about the product, then the algorithm has less confidence in this product's ability to fulfill the customer's needs.

Whereas, if a book comes up in a search query and the customer clicks on the book display to see its product page, the customer sends a signal to Amazon. This signal builds relevance for the book. The increased relevance brings more ability to be served to other customers with similar browsing behaviors and buying patterns. Is this starting to make sense? No? Well, let's keep it going.

Sadly, a few years ago, Amazon became the stomping grounds for bad actors who figured out the ability to build relevance on a product through clicks. So, what did they do? They hired people to search for their product and click the product display to view the product page. Also known as click farms, these groups of bad actors would manipulate the algorithm to favor their products simply through clicks alone.

Thankfully, Amazon was fully aware of this hack and immediately tweaked the algorithm to identify false clicks. In turn, sellers of the products getting the absurd amount of clicks with no sales were banned, and their products were removed. So, before you start thinking the name of the game is to search for your book and click on the product page, don't do it. Amazon will detect false clicks and suppress your book listing and, in due time, remove you from the platform. Then, you will have wasted your time and money on a book about leveraging the power of keywords on Amazon for your books.

Also, it's important to note how Amazon will serve your book up with other relevant publications and their product pages. We'll discuss that in more advanced chapters. Those times are also considered impressions. If someone clicks on the product to view the page, then that click counts toward relevancy. Even if your book isn't showing up when searching, your book might be served through other means, including additional product pages and even Amazon's home page. And, Amazon can share your book through its email newsletter for customers.

So, we know impressions are when customers see your book through a search query, product page, or email. Clicks are when a customer visits your book's product page. The next step in the process and the most critical in building relevance is the sale. Is the browsing customer buying your book when they visit your product page? If not, then you've got a problem.

The most common issue when it comes to not getting a click is a bad book cover. When it comes to sales, if a customer is not buying, then chances are likely your book description isn't on-point. You have to compel the browsing customer into buying your book. But, let's pretend for a minute your book cover and description are on-point. And, let's remove the possibility of window shoppers or people lacking the funds to buy your book.

Why wouldn't a person buy your book? You have a great book cover. Otherwise, they wouldn't be compelled to see more about your book when they clicked on your product. Let's say your book description is on-point. So, why didn't they buy it? Most likely, the keywords you're using are a mismatch with the audience. But, I only adjust the keywords once I've changed the previous elements first. Because if you get sales, then you'll build relevancy for the keywords you have. Unless your keyword choice is so off the wall that they make no sense for your book, then your chances of building relevancy greatly diminishes.

A few other metrics help in determining relevancy for your title. Rather than go exhaustively into each item, I'll focus on a few that make the most difference. These last items revolve around product page engagement. Whatever drives the browsing customer to take action on your page beyond sales is typically a good thing. Unless they click "report abuse." In that instance, you've got a troll on your hands, or you've done something severely wrong.

Engagement comes in a variety of forms, but the biggest and most effective of all is the review. Yep, you should've seen this one coming! When a customer leaves a review on your product page, it builds relevancy for your product. When a conversation happens through comments, it aids in more relevancy. The more consistently the reviews and comments occur on a product page, the more relevant the product becomes.

This is just one example of how author Michael Matthews responds to reviews.

However, I don't encourage you to make review gathering the central part of your business. But, you should make it at least a small piece of your business because the book review works in your favor in two ways:

1. Social proof – third-party credibility goes a long way. Regardless if it's good or bad, a review is proof somebody else experienced your product and took the time to share the experience.

2. Relevance – this small social trigger sends a signal to the algorithm notifying Amazon that people are talking about this product.

However, pay the closest attention to this advice here. Never, under any circumstances, get fake reviews to bolster relevancy for your title. As Amazon identifies bad actors and their dastardly ways, they build automated systems to identify false or biased reviews.

While we're discussing what you shouldn't do with your reviews, avoid getting reviews from people who are not your ideal reader. In the past, I thought you should have your friends and family buy and review your book. I don't subscribe to that belief anymore. Why? Because it messes up the algorithm and begins serving your book through impressions to the wrong audience.

Remember when I had you search for a random product you'd never buy? Then, you got served other similar products despite having no interest? Well, that's what holds true here. If you have your mom leave a review despite her being only a fan of quilting and cat books, then the algorithm is going to think your book should be served to audiences like your mom. This can be a disaster for you, especially if you're publishing werebear shapeshifter books. Your mother's local needle worker's guild might be appalled by the suggestion and immediately click away from your product or ignore it altogether.

Then, your book's one time at bat is a fail; therefore, it drops in relevancy.

As an author who gets reviews, you can decide whether to respond to all reviews or no reviews at all. Yes, that means if you're going to bask in the showering praise of the 5-star reviews, then you need to humble yourself in the mud puddles of 1-star snarky reviews. Treat all reviews professionally and never under any circumstance, get defensive. If you need to get defensive, then don't comment.

Why do you want to comment on a review? Ahem, have you been taking notes or keeping up with me? If so, your guess would've been

– relevancy! Yes, commenting on a review builds relevancy and is 100% acceptable and safe. Again, if you're going to comment on one, you should comment on them all. Just be prepared to take it on the chin. All good authors get low reviews. It's not a matter of "if," it's a matter of "when." Just respond tactfully.

The next action that'll lead to more relevancy for your title is the social share. You'll notice on every product page the ability to share to platforms like Facebook, Twitter, Pinterest, and email. Using those options is a great way to share your product and bring in more customers. You also build relevance for your given set of keywords, especially if a customer brought your book up in a search query. Pretty cool, huh?

Just below the buying options for a product, you'll find the social sharing options.

Lastly is the ability to add a product to a list. Customers can build wish lists on Amazon where they can store items they would like to buy later on. And, this especially becomes great around the holidays because special categories exist for the sake of gift-giving. So, if you have a social following or an email list, recommend that they add your book to their wish list if they can't afford it now.

Amazon Customers can build wish lists by selecting the "Add to List" dropdown just below the buying options for a product.

How Do You Research Keywords?

Now that you have the basis of how keywords function, how exactly do you find the right keywords? And, what do you need for implementing them in the right way? After all, you don't just want to have any old keywords. You also want to have the right keywords that'll bring you more of a buying audience who'll snatch up a copy of your latest book.

The first and most important rule when it comes to keyword research is to never do your research on a naked browser. Yes, I said that with the intention of you thinking what you're thinking. This means you should never do keyword research through your regular browser alone. Assuming you've been on Amazon before, the algorithm is going to tailor search results based on your previous search history and buying patterns. Your results will be significantly skewed, so you should start with a clean slate.

Can we log out of Amazon and hope for the best? Sure, but even then, they'll track your search history as you research.

The best way to start with a clean slate and keep it clean is to use incognito mode. If you're using a Chrome browser, simultaneously press CTRL, Shift, and the letter N when you have the normal browser open. A black browser should appear with a spy logo on the page. If you're using a different browser type, simply Google a way to get incognito mode on your browser.

Head over to Amazon. For ease of research, I highly recommend you bookmark Amazon.com, the Amazon Kindle Store, and the Amazon Book Store. Since you'll be coming to each spot frequently, it's a good idea you save yourself the time of typing it out in your browser every time. When doing keyword research, be sure to research based on the product type. So, the keywords you use on your Kindle ebook should be a slightly different set of keywords than your print books. Why? Relevancy!

Each product brings a different customer type and different tastes. Therefore, the way a print book customer searches content will be slightly different than of a Kindle ebook customer. That's not to say there's no keyword overlap. Some keywords are the same across both publications but don't solely rely on using the same keywords for both products.

Before you attack the Amazon marketplace, I recommend going in with a checklist and a slight game plan. Spend about thirty minutes jotting out various descriptors for your book's content. Nothing is off the table. The more you can describe, the better. If your book is fiction, write out common tropes in your niche, character types, story arcs, settings, and the like.

If your book is nonfiction, write down common problems, solutions, and run the gamut of phrases related to your niche. Remember, folks, nothing is off the table. Now is not the time to allow your inner editor. Don't worry about proper punctuation or how to spell correctly. You just want a checklist of sorts to help guide you through your session.

Let's focus on researching keywords for ebooks. Keep in mind, the steps are the same for print books. Just make sure to use the same list twice, but keep the results separate. If you unearth common keywords in your ebook keyword research, write them down on your checklist for when you do print book research. Now, open your browser in incognito mode and go to the Kindle ebook store. Type in your word, term, or phrase. I recommend starting with just one word. Then, pause.

Autocomplete gives you a better overview of what Amazon customers search on the platform. You'll notice quite a few keyword derivatives built with the root keyword typed in the search box.

The Amazon algorithm is going to get to work and give you common suggestions. A dropdown menu will pop up, showing several keyword phrases with the term you're using as a root keyword. You can do one of two things:

1. Take a screenshot – then use these pictures later for the keyword phrases

2. Jot down the perceived relevant keyword phrases – granted, you're not the algorithm whisperer, so you're going to have to go with your gut. But, you'll know if a term isn't relevant based

1. on if someone asked you about it in a question. Let's say you have a fitness book for men over forty, and you see fitness books for women over sixty. Chances are likely, you won't perceive any relevance with that keyword and your title.

With your browser in incognito mode, the algorithm doesn't know what to serve you. So, it's going to give you broad and generalized suggestions that are most popular. Not all keywords are going to work. In some instances, you might type out a root keyword or keyword phrase that goes absolutely nowhere. A general rule is if the autosuggest dropdown menu populates with at least one keyword, then it's a usable keyword phrase. If not, cross it off your list.

As you go through your original list, you should have a list of more refined keywords. Heck, the list might outgrow your original one. That's okay because the next process is when we're going to separate the studs from the duds. For now, don't worry about guessing if they're proven or not. We just need a list of possibilities. Once you get into the swing of the next few steps, you'll eliminate quite a few of them based on what we find later.

If you start to hit a dead end and need more ideas, use the keyword alphabet concept. Simply type in your root keyword, then hit the space bar. Now, type the letter "A." Wait for the autosuggest. Jot down any relevant keywords. Then, hit the backspace and try "B." Cycle through the whole alphabet to get a long list of keywords. Don't worry, we'll separate out what works best for your title.

Now that you've got a fully curated list, you're going to take all perceived relevant keywords and finally finish the search. So, type in the full keyword and hit Enter. We want to see what Amazon brings back. But, we're not going to settle for just any old keyword.

How many products are pulled up in the search? You'll see this number in the top left corner of the Amazon page. Amazon shows the first sixteen products out of several products. If you see there's sixteen or less products, we might be dealing with a dud. In that case, you can throw out the keyword.

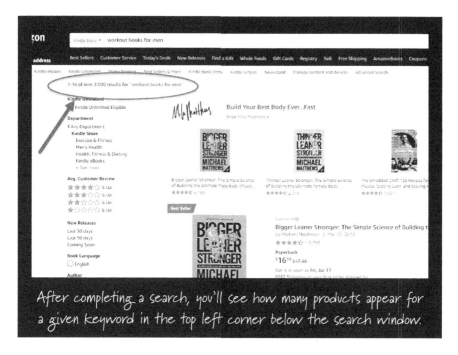

After completing a search, you'll see how many products appear for a given keyword in the top left corner below the search window.

However, if you find a keyword with thousands of products, then you're dealing with a ton of competition. That's not a bad thing! Competition breeds innovation. If you want to be heard above the noise and use a keyword in a competitive market, then you need to lead with your A-game. But, we'll sort out whether it's worth it or not in the next steps.

Generally, I like to see the number of products below 1,000. If you get up to 10,000 products and you're not an established author, you're going to find it hard to place in the first-page search results. It's especially more difficult after launching with no sales and no advertising. When you start getting higher than 10,000 products, cross the keyword off your list. Or, think about expanding on that keyword. Have autosuggest help you.

Let's say the search results for "home workout plan" have 20,000 products in search. Then, we'd go back to the search bar, type in "home workout plan," space, and then use the keyword alphabet method. You should uncover other options that'll get you a more granular, long-tail keyword with fewer search results.

The old adage holds true in that you want to be a big fish in a small pond. As your sales grow, you can expand into other shorter, broader keyword phrases with more products. For now, conquer the small pond until your book gets off the ground and selling regularly.

Now, focus on the first sixteen products served. These are what the Amazon algorithm deems to be most relevant at that moment in time. It should be noted, relevancy is never constant. It's much like an ocean in that waves will come and go. There will be an ebb and flow to all searches. So, you might search for one keyword in one minute and get a particular search volume. But, in the next, you'll get an altogether different set of products. That's how fickle and somewhat unpredictable the algorithm is.

Scroll down the products page. Skip all the ads. You'll know the ads if you see the word "Sponsored" at the top. Focus on the first sixteen products that aren't an ad. Take note on a few things including:

1. Keyword use – focus on the title, subtitle, series name, description, author bio, the editorial section.

2. Reviews – how many reviews does that book have. The more reviews, the tougher it'll be to compete for first-page placement against that book.

1. Publication date – some information is only accessible on the product page. In that case, click on the product and scroll down to the product details.

2. Amazon Bestseller Rank (ABSR) – This is huge, and in no way should you skip past it. The closer the ABSR is to #1, the more the book sells. The further away from #1, the less the book sells.

Towards the end of this book, I'm going to recommend some resources for shortening your research time. However, instead of sounding like some shill trying to push you on products, I'm teaching you the hard and long way of doing things. So, click on the book's product page and browse the product page. Scroll to the middle of the page to view the product details. You'll see the publication date, the ABSR, the customer reviews, and the imprint.

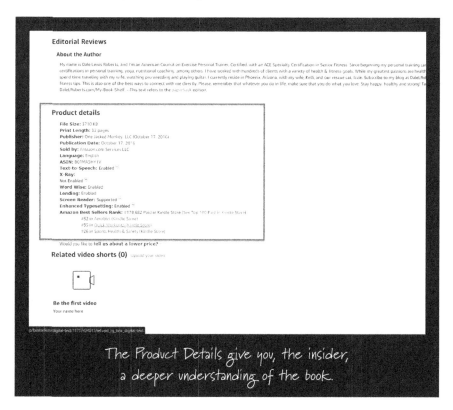

The Product Details give you, the insider,
a deeper understanding of the book.

Fun Fact: If the book's imprint lists "Independently Published," then chances are likely this is a book published through Kindle Direct Publishing.

Keyword Use

If a book has a keyword in the title or subtitle, this publication has nearly cemented the possibility of being pulled up in the search for that term. It doesn't assure it, but it certainly increases the odds. Next, if the book has the keyword in the description, author bio, and editorial section, these are other small triggers building relevancy for this title. Keep in mind, we're not looking for someone who is shoe-horning keywords into every nook and cranny. We're more mindful of what they're doing.

Reviews

As mentioned before, reviews are the lifeblood of social proof and aid in building relevancy. Whether acting as an algorithmic trigger or as a social trigger, reviews play an integral part in proof of concept. If there are a ton of reviews and you plan to share the same shelf space as a book, then plan on catching up somewhat to or competing against this book.

Publication Date

Based mostly on the ABSR, an older publication with a good rank might be proof this book isn't moving anywhere. And, something with staying power is something to model. Do not plagiarize or copy what they're doing. Take notes on common keywords, cover concepts, number of reviews, and more. A book with staying power and decent rank has subtle clues on what you need to do to elevate your book sales.

Amazon Bestseller Rank (ABSR)

This is huge! Generally, I like to see an ABSR under 100,000. To hit #100,000 on the Amazon marketplace, you need at least one sale every day. That's it! Crazy right? With one purchase per day, almost anyone can do it, especially with the right marketing and promotion plan. However, I don't want to see the rank drop below #10,000. Would it be bad if it was closer to #1? No, but again, you're putting yourself into a very competitive niche.

A book with #10,000 ABSR sells about 15 copies per day. That's undoubtedly achievable for most anyone! If you're new, don't fret, you'll get there with persistence and consistency.

> To see an estimate of how many book sales per day it takes to hit a specific ABSR, visit DaleLinks.com/Calculator.

On the first-page search results, I want to see an average ABSR between #10,000 and #100,000. This shows proof of concept. Meanwhile, it also proves with even a soft launch, I should build some relevance on my chosen keywords. I can further cement the relevance for those keywords with an Amazon ad campaign.

Don't feel discouraged if you're finding keywords that are too competitive or not competitive at all. Part of keyword research is going to require intuition. You'll have to go with your gut when choosing. Will you make the best choices as a newbie? Probably not. Trust me, I've gone back to publications I launched in 2014 and cringe at the keyword selection.

The only way to build your intuition is through time and practice. Stick with it, and in due time, you'll find your gut will guide you in the right direction.

Remember the algorithm is ever-changing. Select the keywords you believe best fit your publication at that moment. In due time, you'll want to adjust your keywords if your sales figures aren't quite what you want. However, if your book sales are up and consistent, don't touch your keyword choices. You obviously did something right, so if it isn't broken, don't fix it.

Keep in mind, some keywords are trending and hot in one moment, and no longer of any importance in the next. It had its fifteen minutes of fame, and it's done. I know everyone, and their mother was all over "Apple Cider Vinegar," "Coconut Oil," and "Paleo Diet" in 2014. Now, those topics are hardly pulling in much revenue these days. They've been replaced by "Mindfulness," "Instapot Recipes," and "Keto Diet." Eventually, those will phase out.

Some keywords are evergreen. Rest assured, if it's evergreen, a traditionally published book (trad pub) will typically be at the top of the search. Why? Because they have major advertising, a larger following, and broader reach. So, if you dig around and find a keyword with quite a few trad pub books in the first-page search, then you may want to consider other keyword options.

Not to be confused, you should still check on keywords at least once per year to see if it fits your publication. If your book isn't selling many copies, then you can consider switching out keywords every ninety days. Relevance is variable and ever-changing, but not so much that you want to replace your keyword selections every other day.

When choosing keywords, you're forced to make decisions loosely based on what you see externally. It's hard to tell what a book has done to be successful or get first-page placement. And, even though you may not find your book on first-page placement through incognito mode, it doesn't mean it's not getting served to customers.

Amazon has millions of visitors at any one given moment. They need your product and will serve it to people who seem the best fit. If that doesn't convert a sale, then chances are likely, you'll need to change your approach.

Just don't sweat it too much if you don't see your book pulled up on first-page searches. Somewhere else in some other part of the world, a customer just might be getting your book on a first-page search. The Amazon algorithm customizes the search results based on the customer, not you!

Lastly, before you throw this book across the room and give up on this whole thing, just know it takes time. You aren't going to master this entire thing overnight. And, it will take time and dedication to get your book relevant in the algorithm. In the meantime, do your research and take your time carving out the best choices for your book.

Never guess what keywords go into the seven keyword spots. You're leaving your business to chance, and merely putting in any old keyword off the top of your head will have marginal, if any, results. Friends don't let friends guess their keyword selections.

Once you've got your list whittled down to about 12-24 good keywords, it's time to get to work. As you're researching your keywords, I recommend highlighting any keywords you see as winners. You'll know when it seems right.

As a hypothetical example, I search "YA Science Fiction Romance":

- 250 products

- Average ABSR of 50,000

- Mostly independently published books

- Very few reviews on all books

I'd be all over that and highlight that as a usable keyword.

However, if the same example pulled up this:

- 20,000 products

- Average ABSR 1,000,000

- One trad pub book and the rest are independently published

- Scores of reviews

Then, I'd cross the keyword off the list. There aren't many sales, and assuming the trad pub book is pulling in the vast majority of the sales, then this keyword has low proof of concept. Some keywords might look worth it but prove quickly to be complete flops.

*N*ow that you have a long list of keywords, what do you do with them? If you've already written and published the work, a couple of recommendations won't work out for you. But, the rest are universally applicable. Whatever you do, don't delist and republish a book simply to take advantage of all these tips. Simply adjust what you have and push forward!

Where do you use your list of keywords? We're going to focus on the book's metadata or the information that represents the book that includes:

- Title

- Subtitle

- Series Name

- Description

- Seven Keyword Slots

The prime real estate is going to be in the title and subtitle. But, don't force a keyword into a title if it doesn't make sense. For instance, most fiction book titles won't work having a keyword in them. At one point, people were doing that to gain the favor of the algorithm. Those days are coming to an end. The Amazon customer is becoming more discerning. While the customer wants to read werebear shapeshifter romance books, they don't specifically want a book called Werebear Shapeshifter Romance Book. It's weird, comes off clunky, and reeks of amateur hour.

For nonfiction authors, you have free reign on how you do it. But, be tasteful. Go back to any of my old publications and see how I squeezed as many keywords into the title and subtitle as I could. It worked back then, but now, not so much. Pick the keyword that best identifies your book and slip it into your title or subtitle.

It's believed how using keywords in your title and subtitle greatly increases your chances of first-page placement in searches, but, it's not promised to you. Especially if your book has proven less relevant than other choices. The other thing to be mindful of is other books using the same exact title.

Do not under any circumstances use another book title that's on the market. Don't try to build a deviation or derivative of another title. You're a creative entrepreneur, so the worst thing you can do is stifle your creativity and swipe someone else's intellectual property. If you choose a title and see it's in use, then get creative and pick something different. Language is a beautiful and malleable tool. Bend it how you like to get the best title and subtitle choice that makes sense and can get search traffic.

Before we get any further, you must follow Amazon guidelines when it comes to keyword use. For title and subtitle choice, avoid trademarked names and using other people's intellectual property. For back end keywords, never use any Amazon-based name such as:

- Amazon
- Kindle Unlimited
- Amazon Prime
- And more!

And, the big one is the "F" word – free. Unless your book has context for the word free (and it's not the price of your book), do not use free in your backend keywords. "Dairy-free" or "gluten-free" are examples of when free is allowed. However, Amazon has been known to unwittingly push back on publishers for using "free" in their backend keywords. Sadly, you'll have to state your case and add context as to why you have the "F" word in your keyword slots.

Now that you have a title and subtitle fleshed out, it's time to put some of the other keywords to use in your description. Many would-be experts have long touted that book descriptions are not indexed on Amazon. But, that's the furthest thing from the truth. The process of indexing is when a site places an item as searchable. Just because you have an unheard-of keyword in your description and you can't pull it up in incognito search does not prove book descriptions aren't indexed.[2]

Furthermore, if Amazon didn't index their book descriptions, then at the very least, you would have to account for the end-user – the browsing customer. What better way to validate a browsing customer's search by including keywords relevant to their needs? Organically and tastefully, weave about six to twelve keywords into your description. If you can't get six, that's okay. An excellent book description doesn't always need the best keywords. What it needs is good ad copy that has the browsing customer reading from top to bottom. After reading your excellent description, they should be dying to buy your book.

Keyword Selection + BISAC Choice = Category Placement

When uploading your book to KDP, you'll get to choose two different BISACs. The Book Industry Standards and Communications (BISAC) categories are the internationally accepted categorization for books.[3]

Amazon loosely uses BISAC to help categorize their publications on their platform. If you search the Amazon Marketplace, you won't see a single BISAC category. Why? Because Amazon has its own ways of categorizing. Its categories are there to serve the customer and create a better shopping experience.

Based on the keywords in your book's metadata and the BISAC selection, Amazon then automatically slips your book into categories exclusive to the website. Typically, a category, also known as a browse path, is a mixture of keywords and BISAC, hence why Amazon automatically slips your book into three different browse paths. Behind the scenes, the browse path looks like this:

> Kindle Store > Health, Fitness & Dieting >
> Exercise & Fitness > Ab Workouts

However, the customer-facing category is typically a keyword term describing it like:

> Ab Workouts (Kindle Store)

When you go to a book's product page and scroll down to the product details, you'll see the category selection. Click on it to be redirected to the Amazon Bestseller's list for that category. If you don't see any categories in the product details, then the book hasn't had any sales.

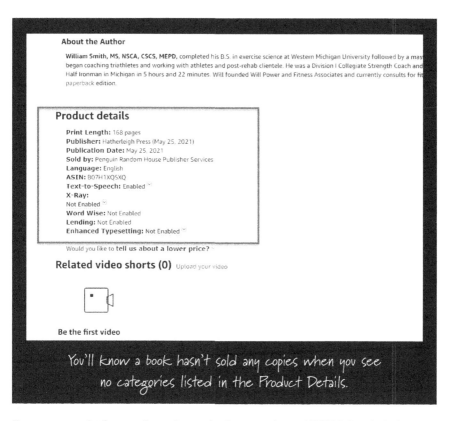

About the Author

William Smith, MS, NSCA, CSCS, MEPD, completed his B.S. in exercise science at Western Michigan University followed by a mas
began coaching triathletes and working with athletes and post-rehab clientele. He was a Division I Collegiate Strength Coach and
Half Ironman in Michigan in 5 hours and 22 minutes. Will founded Will Power and Fitness Associates and currently consults for fit
paperback edition.

Product details

Print Length: 168 pages
Publisher: Hatherleigh Press (May 25, 2021)
Publication Date: May 25, 2021
Sold by: Penguin Random House Publisher Services
Language: English
ASIN: B07H1XQSXQ
Text-to-Speech: Enabled
X-Ray:
Not Enabled
Word Wise: Not Enabled
Lending: Not Enabled
Enhanced Typesetting: Not Enabled

Would you like to tell us about a lower price?

Related video shorts (0) Upload your video

Be the first video

You'll know a book hasn't sold any copies when you see no categories listed in the Product Details.

Bear in mind, if you select the right keywords and BISAC while having a specific type of book, then your book could qualify for invite-only categories. For instance, if you have a short book, you could be eligible for Amazon Short Reads. Again, it's invite-only. However, you can ask to be added to those categories. The worst Amazon can say is no.

Fun fact: I covered Amazon Kindle Short Reads extensively on YouTube. Check out a full video series at DaleLinks.com/ShortReads.

How Do You Fill the Seven Keyword Slots?

After being in the business for over six years, I finally reviewed old titles I published to assess the metadata. Every book needs a good look over and polishing after being on the market for a while. Heck, even the Harry Potter books get a cover change and different descriptions. Your books are no different. I'd recommend evaluating your books more frequently than every six years.

I'm embarrassed to admit I have quite a few titles I haven't touched since my first year in the business. When I reviewed them, I discovered my use of KDP's seven keyword slots was a complete missed opportunity. Each one of the seven slots had one-term keywords - all that space and no real direction.

If you didn't skip forward in the book, then you'll know using single-term keywords for discoverability is not a good idea. You have to expand your keyword phrase and niche down to find your exact audience.

Kindle Direct Publishing allows you seven keyword slots with up to fifty characters per slot. The browsing customer will never see these backend keywords, but hopefully, they'll see your book as a result of using these keywords. These seven keyword slots are a direct line to the Amazon algorithm and a way for you to communicate to it what your book is about. Get it right, and the algorithm will have confidence in your book and build relevance around your selected keywords. Get it wrong, and your book will languish in obscurity.

Not to be confused, the seven keyword slots aren't the be-all, end-all. They're just one metric the algorithm uses in determining the relevancy of your title. This is a missed opportunity for so many authors publishing through KDP.

What do you put in these keyword slots? We already know what you shouldn't put into them, so let's shift gears into what you should put in. Remember your list of vetted keywords? Well, it's time to put those to use.

First, avoid putting your title and subtitle in the seven keyword slots. That's just redundant and won't garner you more search volume. Heck, even KDP says so on their help page.[4] If you have a shared root keyword and build a keyword derivative from the title and subtitle, then that's fine. I encourage you to use different descriptors to get better chances of more comprehensive placement across the platform.

From your list, identify the winners and earmark those for placement in the seven slots. If you found a particularly good keyword with low product results and middle of the road ABSR, then hang onto that for something special.

Find keywords that have overlap. You're looking for keywords with similar root keywords or a shared keyword of sorts. As an example:

- Home workout

- Workout plan

- Exercise plan

- Workout for men

These all share something in common, so I'm going to see if I can build a broad keyword match. Hey, remember the old broad keyword match we talked about towards the beginning of this book? Yep, here's where it's applicable.

The theory is the Amazon algorithm uses the keywords in your seven slots, but it doesn't exclusively rely on exact matches. It focuses more on a broad keyword match. So, this means we can combine a few keywords with similarities in one spot to maximize the little space we have. Then, the algorithm will decipher the words and pick out what makes the most sense to the browsing customer.

In the previous example, we could create one keyword slot from the 4 keywords to read:

> Home workout exercise plan for men

That's not too bad since it has a total of thirty-four out of fifty characters used. We might be able to squeeze in more if it made sense. What you don't want to do is fill the slot with a bunch of unrelated, nonsensical words. That may just confuse the algorithm and waste your slot.

Dave Chesson of Kindlepreneur.com shared a case study where he worked with several books published through KDP. In the study, he ran tests on the seven keyword slots over some time to determine the efficacy of filling a slot versus using exact matches. He concluded that four to six slots were best served as filled to the brim. While the other one to three slots should be an exact match. He did not determine if the order made any difference, so all bets are off there.[5]

So, go through your keyword list:

1. Identify your winners – select about one to three keywords for exact matches.

2. Find overlapping keywords.

3. Combine keywords with overlap for a total of four to six keyword slots.

The most important thing is to review your keywords at least once per year. If sales are going well, then leave them alone. If book sales are horrible after ninety days, then re-evaluate your choices and switch out a few.

The hardest part of choosing and sticking to your keywords is not knowing whether the algorithm deems your book relevant to those keywords. Yes, you can build relevancy with impressions, clicks, buys, and engagement, but how much is enough? Sadly, these are factors outside of our control. The best solution to the lack of relevancy is marketing and promotion. Send more eyes to your product page and get more action going on there. This is a never-ending task, and there's never a day where you can sit back and relax.

Do you ever see brands like Nike, McDonald's, or Coca-Cola stop advertising? No. They pump millions of dollars into advertising, all to continue to be relevant in today's marketplace. The same will go for you as an author. Even cash-strapped authors have options in guest appearances, interviews, in-store signings, speaking engagements, and more. So, no one is immune to doing the work to gain more relevance for their book.

Do not spend every waking hour of your time searching for your book in incognito mode. Just as a reminder, you may not be able to find your book through incognito mode. That doesn't mean someone else isn't seeing your book in their search results. Relax and let the algorithm do its work. You should be worried about promoting your current book and writing your next. Don't sweat an algorithm you have zero control over.

I have one big piece of advice here: keywords don't sell books. Keywords merely make your book more discoverable, that's it! If you have a trash cover and a horrible book description, then no one is going to buy it.

You need to set your ego aside for a minute while I tell you this next piece of advice. If your book isn't selling, it's not an Amazon problem. It's a you problem.

Amazon wants you to succeed and has given you every free tool imaginable to make it happen. If you aren't getting sales, then it comes down to something fundamentally wrong with your book. And, keywords only make up a fraction of the reason why. With millions of customers on the market, I'm hard-pressed in believing your book was never served to several customers on a given day. Facts. It's just a numbers game, and if you aren't selling, then you aren't playing right.

If your book was selling like gangbusters at one point, but has nearly come to a halt, then it's time for you to reassess your keywords, your metadata, and your cover. I'd recommend at the soonest, you change all that out within ninety days. At minimum, assess your keywords once per year. If you have high sales, then leave it alone; you're on the right track.

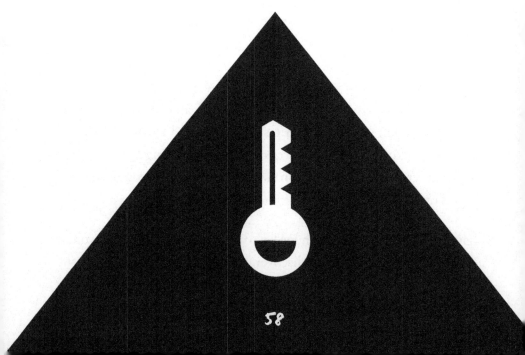

Before diving deep into leveraging the Amazon Advertising platform, it's a good idea we lay the groundwork and set some expectations. I won't be teaching you how to run Amazon Advertising campaigns. There are far more qualified experts you can learn from, so I'll send you to some excellent resources in the back of this book.

Next, do *not* invest any money you cannot stand to lose when advertising. If you're new to advertising, be prepared to lose money upfront. I'm not telling you to just throw money away so you can learn through osmosis. It just doesn't work that way. You'll need to learn from your mistakes and study the data. Running ads requires a highly analytical mind and patience.

The best way to look at advertising is you're going to pay to learn for the first year or so. Once you understand the fundamentals of advertising, you can begin to expand on your knowledge and scale your ads for more discoverability. Just don't expect it to happen over the next few weeks.

The best rule to follow when it comes to Amazon Advertising is to start low and scale slow. Your keyword bids need to be absurdly low (around 10¢ to 15¢ per click), and your daily budget should be nearly the same (around $1 to $10 per day). If you cannot afford to lose $30 to $300 per month, then you shouldn't be fooling with ads. Period.

But, stay with me throughout this chapter, even if you are cash-strapped and Amazon Advertising isn't an option. Amazon Advertising is the most underutilized tool when it comes to uncovering hidden gems and building relevancy. Amazon ads are nearly unparalleled.

When you start to advertise, begin by running a research ad. You'll want to have at least 100 keywords with a maximum of 1,000 keywords. I like to have wiggle room in case I find an exact phrase that I want to add to the campaign. So, I'll usually start an ad campaign above 500 keywords but below 900 total. Then, I can add keywords on an ad as it gains traction.

Your ad should start getting impressions in the first week. The beautiful part is impressions come free. Yep, they're showing your book to the browsing customers for free. Remember, those "Sponsored" book placements in the search results? That's one of many places where it will appear.

Not everyone will pay mind to your ad. The good thing is Amazon Advertising will place your book in front of people. And, one could assume this ad will appear in front of the same person repeatedly. Then, your book cover image and title will work it's way into their subconscious. Eventually, they'll either have to see what you're book is all about or circle back around and search for your book again to purchase it. Pretty neat, right?

It's very much like what Tai Lopez did on YouTube about four or five years ago with his "in my garage with my Lamborgini" video ad. He placed that ad in front of millions of people, and quite a few people (myself included), skipped his ad. It served only as an impression on YouTube Ads. But, after being interrupted so many times, I finally watched the ad in its entirety. Now, I doubt I bought any of his products as a result, but it goes to show he left a lasting impression on me and built his massive online presence through this dumb yet ingenious video ad.

The same can work for you, except without having to flex with your Lambo on customers. These impressions add up over time. It's when you get the clicks that it makes the most difference.

For my research ads, I typically go with broad keyword matches. Once I start getting clicks, the cost will be low, but I'll be able to see what works and what doesn't for my title. Once you get clicks, monitor your "Search Terms" report. It'll show you precisely what the customer searched to get your book as an ad. If you see a keyword that doesn't convert well, you can add it to your negative phrases, so your ad isn't served to anyone using that term again.

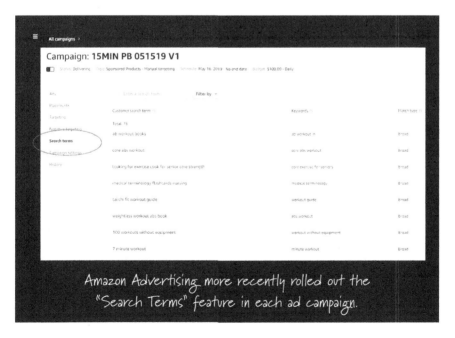

Amazon Advertising more recently rolled out the "Search Terms" feature in each ad campaign.

Conversely, if a keyword converts to a sale, then you need to start building derivative keywords on it in your campaign at the same bid to see if you get more sales. More specifically, you want to take the exact match of the keyword the customer used to convert a purchase and add it to your campaign. Set that keyword as an exact match and bid about 2¢ to 5¢ higher than what it converted at, so long as you are not losing money on the bidding.

A common misconception is if you bid higher on a keyword, you'll get first-page placement. That's simply not true. It comes down to relevancy again. Amazon Advertising will choose the ad that best fits for relevancy, not on the bid alone.

As an example, you have a book selling fifteen copies per day, and I have a book selling one copy per day. You bid 15¢ on a given keyword, while I bid 75¢ on the same keyword. At that given moment, your bid is going to win because your book is a proven commodity. I won't have to pay the 75¢ thankfully, since the winning bid was 15¢. I'll automatically bid below that amount.

Once you understand how Amazon Advertising is like a live auction with clout-based rules, you'll be able to realistically scale. This is why I always recommend you start low and scale slow.

With Amazon Ads, you're going to find some keywords that you win every time. Those are the keywords you should pay the closest attention to and consider using in your metadata if you haven't already. I've found some real gems and seen my sales bump up when adding some of these high-converting keywords. The exceptions to this advice are, of course, author names, trademark names, brands, and the like. Though you can use them in ad campaigns, you still cannot use it in your book's metadata.

If you find a keyword that isn't converting at all and leads to no sales, then make sure to remove it from your book's metadata. It's clearly indicating the audience who uses this keyword in search does not resonate with your product page. Kill it in your description and remove it from your seven keyword slots. It's dead weight.

I highly recommend reading through the Amazon Advertising FAQs[6] and Help[7] section to get a better grasp on how the platform functions best. Also, study Google Ads for a better understanding of how keywords and ads work together.

Amazon Advertising continues to tweak its platform and incorporate a lot of Google Ads principles. One way is how Google does the auction-based system. Google ranks an ad based on a quality score. The way Google scores an ad is based on the landing page experience, the expected click-through rate (number of clicks to impressions), and ad relevance. They further score the quality based on the keywords in the ad, the domain name, and the landing page.[8]

Ultimately, Google will place an ad based on the bid, the quality, and format impact. All that to say, it's not just a platform that sells to the highest bidder. Much in the way Google wants its customers to have a good browsing experience, Amazon wants the same for their customers.

If Amazon doesn't have much confidence in your book, then the ad may not get served often. But, as your book gets more sales and better conversions, then Amazon is more apt to place your ad in a prominent area. And, it's not always about who is willing to pay the highest dollar. Though when it comes to pound-for-pound relevancy, bidding is the next most important metric.

Using Amazon Advertising puts you at a significant advantage over those who do not. You'll get a peek into what customers are searching for and what lead them to become your reader. You're less blind to the customer's journey on Amazon prior to them buying your book. If knowledge is power, then Amazon Advertising is equipping you with the data you need to become a more powerful publisher. Don't take it lightly or for granted.

But, don't hedge all your bets on Amazon Advertising. If you're currently using the platform and losing hundreds on it, then take a step back and study it a bit more. You're probably missing something. I'd recommend reaching out to other peers in this industry who use Amazon ads. Mastermind options and ways to optimize your campaigns. Because, who likes to simply flush money down the drain? I know I don't, and nor should you.

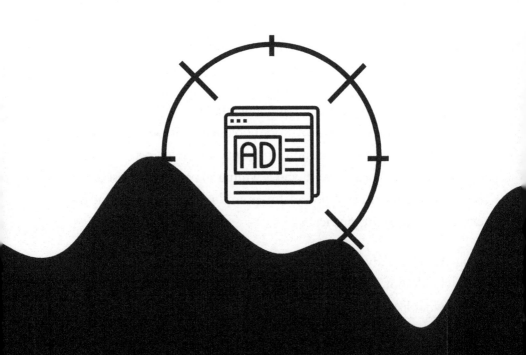

*H*ow exactly do you build relevancy on your title then? We've covered quite a few ways to build relevancy for your title, but it bears worth in repeating. If you can master these ways, then you're off to a better start than most people. Rather than repeating myself, it's best to interweave other tips to build search engine optimization you may have never thought about doing.

The number one way to build relevancy is sales. Nothing builds Amazon's confidence in your product more than cold, hard sales. Anyone who thinks Amazon is merely a political game or how they're favoring only individual books are misled. In an age when ABDL (adult baby diaper lover) absolutely dominates, I can confidently say most any book can. Sure, there are limitations, and you can find out more about the content that KDP does not want you publishing on its platform. Some books simply cannot use Amazon ad campaigns due to their adult nature.

Beyond those few limitations, you should know Amazon wants you to win. After all, if you win, they win. You make money, they make money. But, it can't be an entirely one-sided give and take relationship. What you're willing to take, you have to give somewhat. That's why you cannot merely expect to publish and pray for Amazon to make it a success. Fat freakin' chance. Even *this* book isn't immune to that.

So, what drives sales better than more sales? How do you get more sales? Marketing and promoting. And you must never stop. This is an on-going process that works in perpetuity. You never stop marketing.

One of the best places to advertise is Amazon itself. That's why I'm incredibly bullish about using the Amazon Advertising platform. When using Facebook Ads or Google Ads, you're initially dealing with a cold audience with few exceptions. You're meeting them on another platform where you have to redirect them to your product.

With Amazon, you have a warm audience who are coming to spend money on products. When a customer arrives on Amazon, they're not going to be put off by ads. Why? Because that's all the platform is. It's mostly a search engine that delivers people to products. Amazon has gotten good at interweaving ads in a way that appears seamless. The only indication of it being an ad is where it says "Sponsored." Most customers and outsiders don't even know what that label means.

What it means to you is a customer who's primarily searching for a solution to their problem. Where you'd typically only have your book served for a limited keyword set, you have 1,000 keywords in an Amazon ad. Wow! Who needs seven keyword slots when you are allowed 1,000 keywords in an ad campaign?

As shared before, you don't have to spend hundreds per day to have your book in front of readers. You can start out as low as $1 per day. That's less than the cost of a Starbucks Coffee. I'll pass on the caffeine if that means my book will get in front of people for the next few days.

Will Amazon ads build relevancy for your title? Absolutely. But, it will *not* be the answer to all of your sales problems. If your book has a horrible cover and description, then no ad is going to help solve the issue. Let's face it, selling any product is a numbers game. No matter how ugly your product is or how bad the ad copy, every now and then, you'll get a sale. Your book will hit some customer at the right time who'll forgive a bad cover and won't care about your mistake-riddled book description.

But, what did it take to convert that one sale? How many impressions did it take? How many clicks after that? What is the ratio of impressions to clicks to buys? If it's a lop-sided ratio where you're only converting one in every one-million impressions, then you have an issue.

Amazon Ads are merely plugging a leak in your boat. Sure, every blind squirrel gets a nut once in a while, you cannot view that as the norm. I can guarantee once you stop advertising, your book will go back to languishing in obscurity. That's why it's paramount to pay close attention to the data. Customers will tell you if your book is worth a darn. If it's not selling despite perceived relevant keywords, then you've got a book problem that needs addressing before you can expect better results from your campaigns.

The one time when Amazon Advertising builds more relevancy on your title is when the book is already doing well. It's selling copies like crazy! So, then you add advertising to the mix and boom! You're then running on all cylinders and cooking on all burners.

Speaking of cooking with gas, one of the best ways to enjoy a meal is in the company of friends. And, naturally, when you go to launch your book, you may ask your friends and family to grab it. If you're going against my previous recommendations about friends and family, then I'm going to at least equip you with an easy way to build relevancy.

Instead of sending friends and family to your product page through a link, tell them a keyword, your author name, or the title of your book. Have them visit Amazon to pick up your book with that information.

Yes, you're sending them on a wild goose chase. However, if they're going to be doing your evil bidding, you might as well have them help in search engine optimization.

You could do the same thing when it comes to followers, but I wouldn't recommend it. Don't annoy them or lose out on a potential sale because you wanted to build relevancy for your title.

Sending customers to Amazon equipped with the right keywords to find your book will have them acting like an average browsing customer and selecting your book based on keywords. For every time someone searches for a given keyword, finds your title, and purchases it, that's another action aiding in relevancy.

A few ways to send your readers is by:

- A specific keyword you want to build relevancy for

- Your title and/or subtitle

- Your author name — don't take this lightly. Eventually, you'll build enough relevancy your author name will appear in autosuggest. If you're already published, see if you're appearing there already.

The biggest issue in sending people this way is the fall off. A lot of people don't want to jump through hoops and would rather go right to your page. And, some people won't get the impetus behind you wanting to build more relevance in a search engine. All they hear is, "Me, me, me, me, me…oh, and by the way, me."

It's a big enough task for someone to look for your book, let alone look at it, that it can be a rather tall order asking for them to search for it.

If you do send them on a hunt for your book, at least show them what the cover looks like, so they aren't getting lost. Again, you don't want to frustrate your potential readers. This is why I say this method almost always works out better for friends and family. They're a bit more forgiving.

For followers on social media or subscribers to your email list, give them the link. Don't play around. They just want to get your book and be done with it. Toying with their emotions isn't a good idea. They're bound to wait to get your book another day, if at all. So, give them a direct link.

Never use the long link created from a search on Amazon. Go into your KDP dashboard, find your book, select the region in the drop-down for the publication, and then go there. Use that short link. It'll probably be something like:

```
https://www.amazon.com/dp/B0197JK7Z2
```

You want everyone to buy your book when they visit your product page. That's what will build relevancy. And, if you can, try to be deliberate about when and where you ask. Sending a ton of traffic all at once is suitable for the short term. Still, the algorithm favors consistent performing products versus the short-term trending product. Trickle the traffic, and you'll see much better results.

The next best action to build relevancy is getting more reviews. Review gathering should be part of your regular marketing and promotion strategy. Also, you should add a call-to-action at the end of every book for readers to leave a review on Amazon.

In fact, here's the easiest way to send readers directly to the review page:

https://www.amazon.com/gp/product-review/(ADD YOUR BOOK ASIN HERE)

You merely have to add your ebook or print book's ASIN/ISBN at the end of the link, then you're set. When you first launch your ebook, you won't have an ASIN. So, you'll have to wait until it's launched to insert the full call-to-action. When asking for a review, keep it simple, and do not try to influence their response. Keep it cut and dry like:

Now that you finished reading the book, it'd mean the world to me if you left an honest review on Amazon at (INSERT LINK).

You could add some pizazz to that; however, you get the idea.

I'd recommend sharing posted reviews on social media, in your newsletter, and in future books. Follow it up with a simple call-to-action like the previous one. You could say something simple like:

Have you read (INSERT YOUR TITLE HERE)? If so, it'd mean the world to me if you left an honest review on Amazon at (INSERT LINK). Reviews like this one and yours help me to better craft books and content, so I can make a bigger impact in the world.

The last part was just a random way to share what's in it for them. Plus, it gives permission to your reader to drop feedback and your receptiveness to using it to produce better content.

You'd be amazed at how well this works for low reviews. If you see a one-star review and share it with your following, they'll be quick to drop better reviews to balance out the bad. It's nothing I'd recommend you purposely coordinate since Amazon doesn't like coercion or bias. However, it's definitely a great indirect way to balance out your reviews while building relevancy on your product page.

Of course, remember you can always respond to all book reviews. Keep it professional. Don't respond to some of them and ignore the rest. If you're going to do some, then address all of them. Just don't get defensive.

You get bonus points if you can somehow organically weave in keywords relevant to your book. This is just another way to index your title and validate customer search. It's double bonus points when your readers post a review with your keyword. Again, don't coerce them. That's not a good idea.

The next way to increase relevancy is by asking for friends, family, and followers to share your book through the social media link from your product page. These small social triggers are enough to create small signals to the algorithm and it builds a bit more confidence in your product. One great feature product pages have is the embed feature. You can take a sample from the book and embed it on a website page. This is yet another way to send more traffic to your book.

The embed feature is in the same row as the social sharing features. Only use this option if you're familiar with using HTML coding on websites.

The second most underutilized tool by authors on Amazon is the lists feature. Let your followers know that it's totally okay if they aren't able to buy your books right now. The best way for them to help out and support the cause is by adding your book to a wish list. The nice part is, if they make the wish list public, someone might buy the book for them.

Getting your book added to a list on Amazon helps in your book being placed in additional categories, one of them being "Gift Ideas." You'll most notably see this category surface around the holidays. Do not take this option lightly.

Another highly underutilized tool by authors on Amazon is Author Central. Amazon equips authors with a profile page at no additional cost. And, the beautiful part is this page is another way to index your books and share from one spot. So, rather than sending your followers to any one book's product page, you can send them to your Amazon Author Profile.

An Amazon Author Profile further indexes your catalog and gives readers a place to find all your books.

Also, having an Amazon Author Profile makes your author name a clickable link on your book's page. Once a customer clicks on your author name, they'll be whisked away to your author profile where they'll get to see other books by you. This, in turn, builds more awareness of your other titles. There's also a sweet little "Follow" button located below your author picture. When a visitor clicks on that, Amazon will notify them when you release your next book. Though the notifications are a bit delayed, it still helps for little bursts of sales after a book launch.

Author Central has several neat features, but the biggest ones include: all your reviews curated in one spot, editorial reviews, and historical sales ranking. The latter option is useful if you obsessively camp out on your product page. If you do camp out there, I'd recommend you move to Author Central. The issue with hitting refresh on your book's page is it slowly erodes the relevancy of your title since you are not buying the book. Though this is merely a theory, it's not one I'm willing to test since Author Central tracks your Amazon Bestseller Rank.

> Fun fact: A few years ago, I shared a comprehensive overview of Amazon Author Central. Take a look at the video series at DaleLinks.com/AuthorCentral.

One last way to build relevancy is an indirect feature made available through the magic of Amazon. It's the "Also Bought" and "Frequently Bought Together" features on a product page.

Amazon customers are notorious for buying more than one product per transaction. So, Amazon made it simple for other customers to see what previous customers have bought in tandem. Nothing attracts a crowd like a crowd. When other customers notice another product was purchased along with the current product they're considering, they're apt to either:

A. Check out the other product – if that other product is your book, yay! If not, boo hiss!

B. Buy both products.

Quite a few customers used to buy a number of my fitness books together or with other fitness author's books.

You typically will only see this feature on products that have been on Amazon for a while. This is not a feature you'll see on the first day of launch or during pre-orders. Why? Because Amazon is stating a fact when it says these items are frequently bought together.

You'll find the "Customers Who Bought This Item Also Bought" and a row of selections on most ebook listings. For print books, it'll say

"Frequently Bought Together" where it'll show your print book listed with other print books including a total cost of both together.

"Frequently Bought Together" is a great feature for customers and an excellent insight for you, the author.

"Also Bought" and "Frequently Bought Together" is why I discourage marketing and promoting to friends and family. Unless you have someone close who is your ideal reader (sorry, your mom doesn't count), asking them to buy your books is going to mess up this feature. It just confuses the algorithm, and if you do it bad enough, you'll end up in some weird combinations.

Will it kill your relevancy having friends and family buying your books? It's certainly debatable. Rather than be saddled with the heartache of cleaning up your "Also Boughts" and rebuilding your book's relevancy, it's best to err on the side of caution.

Is there any one thing that could kill relevancy for your book? Yes. Complacency. I can assure you after allowing my fitness brand to sit unattended for over three years, those books' better days are behind them. Though it was not my sole source of income, it was undoubtedly the main contributor in my early publishing days. If I had to do it all over again, I would've assigned a manager to promote those assets. That would've mitigated any loss in relevancy.

I'd recommend the same to you. To maintain a strong foothold on Amazon, you need to have a consistent marketing and promotion plan to keep your book's relevancy high.

When you're hard-pressed on running ads, then follow the old adage prolific author and co-host of 20BooksTo50K, Craig Martelle says:

> Nothing sells your last book like the next book.[9]

So, when forced to do the next best thing, write your next book and keep pushing forward.

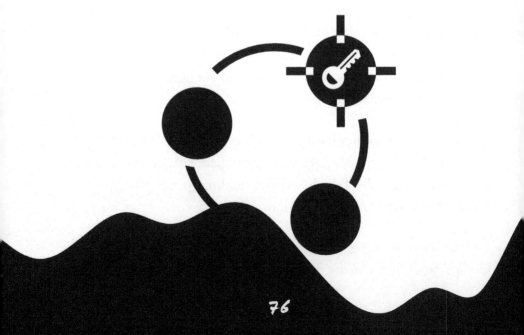

Well, now that you learned it all the hard way, I'm going to give you a few ideas for tools to consider to add to your arsenal. Some tools come at a premium, and others don't cost a dime. Of course, some of my preferred tools are free, but I have one that I don't go without, and it does cost a premium.

Publisher Rocket

Publisher Rocket is a premium tool with four different features: Competition Analysis, Category Research, and the two most essential tools, the AMS Keywords Finder, and the Keyword Research Tool. The last two options alone are worth the $97 investment I made three years ago.

Rather than spend hours trawling about on Amazon for relevant keywords, Publisher Rocket does it all in a matter of minutes. And, the best part about Rocket, is how you see the estimated number of searches per month and a competition score. Getting to see the estimated searches per month is a game-changer, and it gives you a better overview of how a keyword performs beyond just the ABSR, number of products, shelf-life, and reviews.

The second feature, the AMS Keywords Finder, makes creating Amazon Advertising campaigns a cinch. You simply type in a keyword relevant to your title, and Rocket comes back with hundreds of relevant keywords. My best campaigns were run using the Rocket AMS Keywords Finder.

I'd recommend if you use this feature for ads, grab your seven backend keywords to build a list. If you have to break down some keyword combinations, do that before you run a report with Rocket.

Believe it or not, this book went through three different versions. This version is the product of a complete overhaul and rewrite. In the last two versions, I leaned heavily into how much I loved this tool. But, I was afraid it'd turn off readers and make them believe it was merely a book meant to sell Publisher Rocket licenses.

When reflecting on my career over the past six years, the first three years I went without any tools. Yeah, the first two years were tough as hell, but if it weren't for learning the fundamentals of keywords, I wouldn't be able to share the information in this book nor carve out a career as an indie author.

So, rather than gushing over Publisher Rocket anymore, I'd recommend you watch my video review about the product at DaleLinks.com/RocketReview so you get a better overview. Or, you can head to my affiliate link at DaleLinks.com/Rocket for more details.

Kindlepreneur

Okay, I'm not gonna lie. You could literally throw this book in the trash in front of me if you agreed to go straight to Kindlepreneur.com. This is one of the best resources online today when it comes to understanding the business of self-publishing! Run by indie author and self-publishing expert, Dave Chesson, Kindlepreneur is the self-publisher's

Self-publisher. When indie authors have a problem, they typically reach out to Dave for the answer.

Flip to the back of the book to get a full list of articles I find the most informative. Any post written by Dave is meticulous and well crafted while staying simple enough to read in one sitting.

DS Amazon Quick View

This Chrome browser extension is a godsend and doesn't have to cost a dime. Heck, I've used the free version for the past couple of years and don't know how I functioned without it. Remember, how I had you painstakingly research your keywords and click on each product page to scroll to the product details for the ABSR, publication date, and reviews? Well, you get to see that all in the search results.

Before you start researching next time, install DS Amazon Quick View into your browser. Then, enable the browser extension for incognito mode. Simply go to your browser settings, then go to your extensions. Now, find DS Amazon Quick View. Then, enable it for incognito mode.

You're all set then. Next time you're doing research, you'll see a gray box below the books in the search results. It'll show the ABSR. Hover your mouse over top of the book cover to reveal the product details.

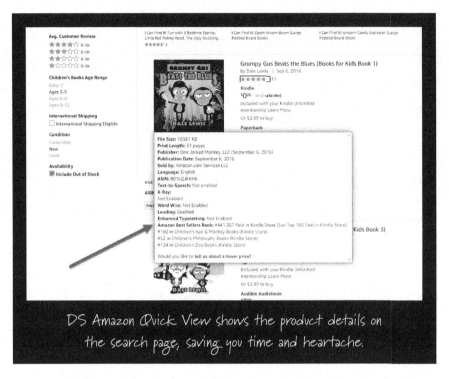

DS Amazon Quick View shows the product details on the search page, saving you time and heartache.

DS Amazon Quick View is simply the best tool you can find for considerably shortening your keyword research time. Sorry in advance if you did hours of research only to discover this option. Again, I didn't want to seem like a complete shill for all these products.

Understanding Search Engines

If you really want to master the game of self-publishing and keyword use, then you need to get a better understanding of search engine algorithms. I invested thousands into books, videos and courses to learn what I know. And, I hate to tell you, this doesn't even scratch the surface. If a search engine programmer read this book, they'd lose their mind at how much I minimized the work they put in.

The areas you'll want to focus on are Google, YouTube, Facebook, Instagram, Twitter, and of course, Amazon. Getting the right information is easier than you know. You've already made it through this book, so you clearly have the aptitude for learning about keywords. I'd assume you'd be willing to learn even more, especially if you're a self-starter.

Rather than plunking down a ton of money, I'd recommend a few free resources to start you off. First of all, YouTube is your friend and can bring you back a ton of free content. I've found some of the best free content on YouTube. Just be picky about who you learn from. If someone is flexing with their Range Rover on you, then chances are likely, they aren't trying to teach you, they're trying to fleece you. Run away. However, someone who's been in the writing community for a while may have your best interests at heart and won't give any misinformation.

Other places to grab great info is your local library. Believe it or not, there are lots of print books, ebooks, and audiobooks designed to teach you more about search engines. I'd say pick a platform and run with it. Amazon is a good place. If I'd recommend any other, it'd be Google or even YouTube next.

Also, some libraries are enrolled in a course platform called LinkedIn Learning formerly known as Lynda.com. If you have a library card, all you have to do is sign in with your library card, and you can get scores of free courses! It's ridiculously good and doesn't cost you a dime. The library and LinkedIn foot the cost so you can elevate your education.

You can also keep an eye on platforms like Udemy or Gumroad for free courses or digital downloads. It's funny, but I don't believe you need to invest more than just a little time and a willingness to learn when it comes to understanding search engines.

*A*fter an hour of chatting about pro wrestling with Dan, Andru, and Mike, we dispersed and moved onto other conversations in the crowded room. I don't think any of us were anymore introverted than the other, but having that common ground gave us enough to get warmed up and the courage to chat with other people about anything else besides pro wrestling.

It's funny how the situation would've been different had the four of us not had that common ground. How would the conversation have gone? Would our random visitors have stayed longer? Or, would they have not even stopped by to chat in the first place? After all, nothing attracts a crowd like a small group of guys loudly and enthusiastically professing their love for a strange business that's been labeled "fake" by outsiders.

Imagine how stilted the conversation would've been without that common ground. What would we have talked about? Would we have all gone our separate ways and called it a day? Or, would we simply grind it out and find the right conversation in due time?

Keywords are organically woven into the fabric of conversation. We just never call them keywords. We call them interests, topics, passions, dreams, and the like. When you can draw a parallel between real life and business based around a machine, you bring a more human element that ties humans together.

After all, we're not selling books to machines. We're selling books through a machine to other human beings. When you can attach an emotion to what you're doing and acknowledge the person on the other side of the transaction, you'll both win in the end.

So, as you do your keyword research, upload your selected keywords, and run a campaign with keywords, remember you're not doing it for an algorithm. You're doing it to build a bridge between your book and your ideal reader. To better state it, you're starting a conversation with someone who shares the same interests as you. And, hopefully, you draw a crowd and grow a kinship in the process.

PROMOTIONAL STRATEGIES
for
BOOKS

HOW TO MARKET & PROMOTE YOUR BOOK

Contents

Rejection is a hard pill to swallow. To make matters worse, it was my eighteenth birthday. Usually, you'd think this was a monumental event. After all, it was the day I officially became a man. Everyone wants to share in this big day, and I was no different. This day teemed with errors and oversights. It all came down to me, who I knew, and how I made others aware of my birthday celebration.

Not to sound like a complete ingrate, I was thankful to spend my birthday with my mother. She was kind enough to be there for me on my big birthday and went out of her way to buy a half sheet of birthday cake and the essentials. My mother even drove half an hour out of her way to ring in my birthday. She was the only person to celebrate with me.

Being far away from home and having very few friends growing up did me no favors. The few people I knew from my hometown were merely one block away in another dormitory. I felt a certain kinship to them since we came from such a small town. I often questioned if this feeling was mutual and soon found out it wasn't.

All I had to do was invite people to my birthday, the place to meet (my dorm room), and get a general headcount. It seemed like I had everyone I knew on board, including the hometown acquaintances and a few new friends. I expected at least a dozen or more people. That's not too bad and was more than sufficient for an intimate celebration.

The time came, and my mother was already there with bells on. I waited for my friends to stop by and hang out with them. We could scarf down a tasty cake while chatting about our newfound college life.

That time never came. No one showed. Five minutes passed, and I figured they were simply on their way. Ten minutes passed, and I grew a bit concerned about their well-being. Fifteen minutes passed, and my mother began to think the half sheet might have been an overspend. Finally, I mustered up the nerve to call my expected attendees. A few of the phones remained unanswered. Once I finally got one person on the phone, I mentioned it was my birthday and wondered if he was still coming.

To my surprise, he wasn't aware of the celebration. Though, looking back, I don't believe there was any shock on his part. It was more how he tried to cover his tracks. The guy didn't want to come, but he wrangled the few stragglers from our hometown, and they slowly moseyed over to my dorm room. No sooner had my mother dished out their cake, they all inhaled it, said the obligatory "happy birthday," and left quicker than they came. Most of the cake remained intact, along with my shattered confidence, self-esteem, and emotions.

Keeping a brave face on, I thanked my mom for coming. When we parted ways, she left the large remaining portion of cake as a reminder of my failed attempt at my first birthday celebration in adulthood.

Launching a book is much the same way. As an author, you laboriously toil away at a manuscript. You've spent all your time, energy, attention, and money into this love of yours. It's remarkable, and why not? It's a piece of you that you want the world to share. It's a milestone all your friends, family, acquaintances, and even strangers should share in.

Yet, what do you do when no one shows to partake in your work? More specifically, how do you get more people to read your book? What do you need to do beyond writing that'll get people to buy and read your book?

What I conveniently didn't share with you in my story was the lack of preparation I had. Also, I didn't do a good enough job in communicating how important this celebration was. And, while my hometown buddies shared a little in common with me, they didn't share enough in common to make it worth their while to eat cake with someone they didn't feel particularly fond of. After all, college parties were more about keg stands and beer bongs, not sugary cake and fruit punch. I had a complete disconnect with my audience and failed to build awareness around the event.

The failed birthday party was on me, and so is a failed book on the author. If your book isn't doing well, it's on you. It's not on your audience. It's not on the platform that distributes it. The ultimate success of your publication relies solely on your ability to market and promote it. It doesn't just start days before the publication date. Marketing and promotion don't end once your launch date comes. They're unending tasks if you ever want to see consistent success in your publication.

Rather than writing and publishing your next book to an audience of crickets, you're going to learn how to solve that problem ASAP. There'll be no more pity parties for your book launch. Forget about making your mother the only recipient of your book. We're going to help troubleshoot your lack of book sales while offering up sensible and practical steps for marketing and promoting your book to the moon and back. With every launch, you'll get more and more people.

In due time, your audience will hit critical mass, and you'll look back on your previous missteps fondly like I do about my sad eighteenth birthday party. Let's dig into this tasty dessert known as *Promotional Strategies for Books*, and get you fast on your way to your book's greatest successes! The good news is you won't have to eat any extra calories or do any keg stands to get there. See you on the next page!

*Y*ou may have heard this phrase thrown around time and again, but do you truly know what marketing and promotion mean? Though each is mentioned one with the other, they both play a slightly different part. However, one doesn't function well without the other. If your marketing is off, then your promotional efforts won't amount to jack. And, if your promotional strategies suck, then your marketing will be all for naught.

Marketing boils down to the overall appearance, viability, and accessibility of your brand. It's how consumers (also known as the market) view you, your services, your product, and your overall brand. If you don't put any time or effort into who your audience and their expectations, your marketing sucks. However, if you get to know your ideal reader and their needs, then your marketing plan is bound to be off to a much better start.

Before you even publish your work, it's important to dial in for whom you are writing. Here are a few questions to consider:

1. Who is your ideal reader?

2. What is your ideal reader's problem?

3. What does your ideal reader expect from your book?

4. What has your ideal reader come to expect from your niche?

When considering these questions, track down successful authors who've already walked the path you want to travel. Now, pay attention to these few items:

- Cover design — How does it look? What's the tone? Is it the same as the others in the niche?

- Content — What's the writing style? Is it something you can do? Can you create something similar?

- Content length — How long is the content? How many pages?

- Reviews — What are readers saying about the book? What is missing from that book you can fulfill?

What a lot of authors fail to realize is marketing comes down to not just the content, but the outward appearance of that content and the way consumers perceive that content. Get it wrong, and no one will be interested. Get it right, and you're fast on your way to realizing success.

Once you nail down your marketing plan, what do you do to get your product seen? You promote it. This is the least sexy part of the business. Everyone loves to write a good book. Most everyone loves to get a stellar book cover for their publication, but few people like to promote their book. Why? Because it's not easy.

What stands in our way of selling more books and success is one simple concept – rejection. When only a few people buy your book, it seems like the world is rejecting your work. That sucks! No one likes rejection, much less the failure of never realizing success for all your hard work.

You're probably saying, "Dale, I don't have an issue with rejection."

Really? Then, what have you done to promote your book lately? How many sales did it garner? If it was a small number, how did you feel about it? It probably felt bad, almost the same feeling you get when someone rejects you. However, the good news is if you find a promotional strategy that works, no matter how small, then you've seen enough proof of concept to try it again. You'll just need to refine your approach or tweak your marketing to get better results.

To cement my argument about how authors don't like to market their book, I'll break down exactly what promotion is. When you promote your book, you're essentially sharing who you are, where you're at, and what you do. It leaves you in a vulnerable position. That's why it's never nice to have little to no results when promoting your book.

What we have to do is refine your approach to marketing and promotion. If you *only* get your brand on-point and your promotional plans dialed in, then you significantly increase your odds of success. Though you might feel strong in one area of marketing and promotion, I implore you to read all the way through and don't skip the content. I have a ton of information that'll start with the fundamentals and build up to more advanced tactics.

Without knowing what you should do to start, advanced strategies will never help you grow your author brand or sell more books. Quite a few authors get that wrong. You can't learn to fly until you learn the basics of how to crawl. First, let's undo some misunderstandings and exercise critical thinking about marketing and promoting books.

*A*fter six years of self-publishing and four years of teaching people how to do it, I've heard many of the same excuses for low book sales. I can usually track it back to bad marketing and promotion. Let me rephrase that for emphasis. Authors are not successful because they are not marketing and promoting their books properly.

When authors do a particular marketing and promotional strategy right, they drop the ball in another area – consistency. You must be consistent in your marketing and promotional efforts to see any real results. The business of self-publishing is a long game. Forget all the get-rich-quick dreams some random online hack has sold you. Dismiss any random interview you saw of an author who made $10,000 in their first 30 days. The vast majority of authors have to work their faces off to get anywhere in this business. And, they have to do it consistently over time to see any results.

Woody Allen once said, "Showing up is eighty percent of life." But, showing up just isn't enough to make an impact. You have to show up one hundred percent of the time consistently to see real results.

In fact, the old quote from Bruce Lee states it best when he said:

> I fear not the man who has practiced 10,000 kicks once, but I fear the man who has practiced one kick 10,000 times.

Bruce wasn't merely referring to martial arts. He focused more on what people do to achieve success. It goes beyond just doing one thing many times at one time. Success in business boils down to how much you put in consistently over time. So, if you want to achieve any modicum of success, you must commit to it, stick to it, never let up, and keep pushing forward.

All of this applies to marketing and promotion. It's not enough for you to put pen to paper and publish the content. If you expect anyone to find your work, you need to put in the most work after you've published your content. After all, publishing and praying alone will only get you so far. The whole process of marketing and promotion should begin well before you even put pen to paper.

When Should an Author Begin Marketing and Promotion?

What came first – the chicken or the egg? This analogy seems to play a huge part in determining when authors should begin marketing and promotion. Quite a few authors believe you can't be successful until you've published a book or a certain number of books. Then again, you can't get anyone to read your book unless you have a following either, right? Yes.

Even though you can leverage keywords to gain more discoverability on Amazon, you shouldn't rely solely on Amazon to do all the hard work for you. The fact is you are going to have to do 99.9% of the work, and it all starts right now. Whether you're a new author or a veteran self-publisher, it's up to you to build your following. But where do you start? How do you get a following if you don't have a book? Stay with me, because it's going to take some time to give you a full overhead view of what to do and where to go.

It's not as simple as saying:

> Do X, Y, and Z, and you'll be good to go.

There are far too many moving parts, so we'll have to chip away at this one swing at a time. In the meantime, know that marketing and promotion should start before you even put pen to paper. The hype train leaves the station as soon as you've internally committed to writing a book. That's all you need to know for right now.

Once you get started, publish your book, and you promote the launch, when do you stop? You stop once you've had enough. Famous brands like Nike and McDonald's never stop marketing and promoting. Why? They want the top spot as the foremost authority in their niche. These brands want to be the only viable option in athletic wear and fast food, respectively. You want the same for your book.

In fact, in an interview with a business strategies consultant, Jonny Andrews, I asked if one book was enough. He essentially said it is, but the promotional work is going to be far heavier than if the author had an entire backlog to send people to. That means if you decide to publish only one book, you'll need to put all your time, energy, and attention into building awareness around that book. The work never stops.

Should an Author Ever Stop?

In 2019, I faced the scary reality of what happens when I don't promote my books. I have a backlog of over forty different books in health and fitness, with thirty-eight titles translated into seven other languages. This brand of fitness books crushed it from 2016 to 2017, but it slowly died away. Why? Because my attention went elsewhere, and I stopped actively promoting these titles. Where these books had been pulling in substantial revenue, now they were hardly making any significant profits.

I discovered first-hand what comes from sitting back on my laurels and expecting the world to come to me. To my credit, I consciously walked away from the fitness brand in 2018 to focus on my career as a video content creator. I even admitted to myself I didn't care if the books died off. In reality, and subconsciously, I believed these books would continue to pull in the lion's share of the revenue.

When your product doesn't perform consistently or draw in enough sales on Amazon, the algorithm focuses on other products that will sell. Where my fitness books pulled in significant revenue at one point, other books since replaced them and made up for the loss in revenue. My books fell out of grace with the Amazon algorithm.

Momentum vs. Inertia with Marketing and Promotion

In 2016, my fitness brand was on fire. It seemed I could do no wrong with the Amazon algorithm. Heck, I didn't even have to touch Amazon Advertising at the time. I solely relied on external sources such as free book promotion websites, email marketing, and social media marketing to drive traffic to my books. Going into 2017, I stopped consistently promoting my books. I even gave up on using KDP Select for promoting my titles and decided to publish beyond the Amazon platform so I could gain more readers.

Though momentum worked in my favor from 2016 to 2017, the following year came with force equally powerful as momentum. It was inertia. That means my book sales slowed down and even came to a near halt. Trying to get momentum back in my favor would be a near-impossible task. Why? Because it's like I'm starting from scratch, except worse. The Amazon algorithm loves new products. It also loves proven products. To get back into the good graces of the Amazon algorithm, I'd need to prove myself all over again.

Much like pushing a giant snowball uphill, it'd be tough, but it wouldn't be impossible.

I gave each of my fitness books a facelift, changed the book descriptions, added a few new keywords, and then fired off new Amazon advertising campaigns. In truth, though, I'm merely using these books as a case study and a testing ground. As you can imagine, since you're reading a book about self-publishing, my direction is no longer with the fitness brand. Instead, I'm focused more on building the *Self-Publishing with Dale* brand. Rather than go back to something of mild interest, I'd rather pay the closest attention to what I can stick with for the long term. That means marketing and promoting consistently for the next few years and beyond.

I share my story to demonstrate the power of momentum versus inertia. The effectiveness of your marketing and promotional efforts relies heavily on whether you have momentum in your favor or if you're working against inertia. That's not to say you should quit if you have inertia working against you. It's merely to state you might have one heck of a hill to climb if you want to get anywhere with your promotional efforts. The best part is if you set up an author platform, it's much easier for you to keep the ball rolling and momentum working for you.

After the launch of Kindle Direct Publishing (KDP), the world's perception of self-publishing forever changed. No longer was self-publishing relegated to conversations surrounding your weird uncle who wrote, published, and bought a pallet-full of erotica books in his garage. Self-publishing became accessible to everyone. Authors who would otherwise get rejected by traditional publishing companies and agents could now skip the gatekeepers and publish their work themselves.

As the walls came crumbling down and ebooks stepped to the fore-front of publishing, a new crop of entrepreneurs stepped up. Quite a few of them had the best intentions and are still running profitable self-publishing businesses. Simultaneously, another lot of get-rich-quick schemers and scammers saw the land of opportunity and loop-holes to abuse in the system.

Since the Amazon algorithm could be used and abused, these bad actors found a way to publish content onto the Amazon platform quickly. They could easily fleece buyers of their money by putting out low-quality content with no real direction and the sole intent of making money. These efforts were at the expense of the customer.

As Amazon KDP matured, the algorithm and systems became more sophisticated. KDP closed loopholes abused by the bad actors. Nat-urally, as these bad actors saw they could no longer simply shotgun out dozens of books in a week based on various topics, they closed up shop and moved to the next big thing.

Meanwhile, authors who established themselves early on saw a big return on their early efforts. These authors wrote high-quality books, nurtured a growing readership, and focused on delivering value to their audience. These authors had momentum working in their favor and not merely loopholes that rewarded them.

What set these authors apart from the rest was how they stuck to it. They built a lasting presence and continued to do it despite all the changes through Amazon KDP. They created what is called an author platform, or I sometimes call it a brand.

An author platform is so much more than just a stage where an author speaks to his fans. It's a consistent message and placement of the message that makes up the author platform. The author platform can consist of:

- What readers expect

- Where they can find the author

- How they can rely on that author

- How they perceive the author

- When readers can expect to see the next release

The author platform can be as simple as:

- An author website

- A marketplace to buy their books

- Social media presence

- Any miscellaneous ways readers can find the author

- Places where the readers can interact with the author—online forums, social media, etc.

The authors who confidently march forward into battle and never let up are rewarded in the long term, so long as they stay true to their author platform and brand. If they don't deviate from their mission, stay true to their audience, and consistently promote their platform, they'll win big. We're in the age of the brand and author platform. Amazon loves to reward authors who put in the work and bring in the audience. Nothing attracts a crowd like a crowd. The only way to draw in that crowd is to build an author platform.

Where do you start building an author platform? How do you build a brand that lasts? What are the first best steps to establishing your author presence?

Building a brand seems simple in theory, but in practice, it's much harder to fire off. Before you can ever consider making any significant impact on your author earnings, you need to consider the impact you'll make in the world.

In *Amazon Keywords for Books*, I shared how my first book was my worst book. To say it was hammered garbage is mildly offending to dumpster fires throughout the world. I believed I wrote a book for everyone. Once a friend opened my eyes to the error of my ways, I found I'd written a book for no one. Because when you try to please everyone, you please no one in the process.

Before you write your next book, I want you to consider a few things:

1. Who is your audience?

2. What is your message?

3. How is your message relevant to your intended audience?

4. Can your audience rely on you to be steadfast in what you provide?

Imagine visiting your local shoe store to pick up some new footwear. Your expectation when you arrive is you'll browse the selection of shoes, find what you're looking for, try on a few pairs, and then hopefully buy something. What if you showed up to your local shoe store only to discover they're now selling pizza? No, they don't sell shoes, even though their name would imply otherwise. No, they won't make a special order for you, because they're no longer selling shoes. If you want pizza, they're your place. If you want shoes, well, you're out of luck.

When you go to a shoe store, you expect to buy shoes. That's how a brand works. A brand is an unwritten promise with the world of what you deliver and what they can expect. If you can't get good on that promise and stay consistent with what they've come to expect, you're in real trouble.

Your brand is essentially your promise. It boils down to:

- Your appearance

- Your message

- Your core values

- Your deliverables

Brand-building is now more critical than ever because we're in the age of technology. Search engine algorithms dominate our lives online. If you want your audience to hear you above the online noise, then you need to build a brand. Your brand's message needs to be consistent across the board.

Much like I shared how Amazon rewards consistent performing products, most search engines do the same. If you're the expert and go-to authority in underwater basket weaving for dolphins, then stick to it. After you've been at it for a few years and have consistently promoted your brand, then you'll earn the favor of most any search engine.

Where do you start? What are the things you need in place? Well, you need to know who you are. For simplicity's sake, let's focus on you as an author. Your author name should be prime real estate when it comes to building a brand. Whether you're using a pen name or your given name, this is probably the best step forward.

The first step you need to take is to own all properties containing your name. That means you need to take your virtual flag and place it in the sand on a website domain name and throughout social media. Even if you don't plan to use social media, you still need to take it. You're planning for the next five years. If you're working with my plan, then that includes going big or going home. We go big every time. Take the social media handles; that way, it safeguards you later when bad actors try to impersonate you.

Bad news if you're name is Michael Johnson (sorry, Uncle Mike, but it's true) – it's going to be tough finding just the right domain name and social media presence. If you're an author, then chances are you have creativity on your side.

Choosing a Domain Name & Social Media Handles

I can hear the collective groan from some of you. Yep, getting a website is mission-critical for establishing your brand. Part of having and running a professional website includes having an author-specific domain name. No, you're not going to rely on free hosting with Wix and their unmemorable long URL. I take no issue with free site hosting, but you need to make it easy for any reader to discover you or find you after reading your book. They can't find you if your web address is MichaelHJohnsonHotAuthor.Wix.com. At that point, you're promoting Wix's brand, not your author brand. No offense to Wix, but I'm not in the business to promote Wix when building my author brand.

The next thing to consider is social media names, also known as handles. If you skip this part, I promise you will regret it later. Eventually, as your author brand picks up steam, you're going to have some random person take your name. And, in some instances, they might even assume your identity and impersonate you. It sucks! So, safeguard your brand, and your future self will thank you.

What social media platforms will you need? It depends a lot on where your audience is. Rather than getting hung up on the details, I'd recommend you reserve as many of them as possible. Just be sure to use all the same login names and store all your passwords safely.

Visit NameCheck.com to find out the availability of your brand name. I've used this site quite a few times to help coaching students reserve their names. It's free to use and will quickly show you where your name is available. You simply type in your name and press Enter to see what is or is not available.

My primary concern is if the domain name is available. I'd recommend keeping your domain name simple. Do not complicate it with acronyms, numbers, or symbols. You need a domain name that's is easy to say and remember. For example, my author name is Dale L. Roberts. Naturally, readers will recognize my name from my book as Dale L. Roberts. My domain name of DaleLRoberts.com is simple and easy to remember. That's what you want to do.

A coaching student once reserved a complex domain name having little to do with her author name. Heck, it wasn't even a word, but more of an acronym for something that seemed like an inside joke. It went something like ADFXBooksToWeightLoss.com. Insert my perplexed look here. Confused by the name, I asked her what it meant. She explained the meaning behind the name and was confident readers would remember it. Nearly three years later, this author hasn't gone anywhere with her brand. Why? She hedged all her bets on a name no one would remember, much less know.

If you're shooting for using your author name and it's taken, then try different variations of your first, middle, and last name. Try to add "the" or "author" as a prefix in the domain name. It's going to take time. Once you've found a good domain name, reach out to any number of domain name registrars online. You can usually find a domain for about $17 per year. Choose your service provider wisely and check their reviews before investing your money in them.

Now comes the social media aspect of things. It's okay if you can't get your domain name to precisely match your social media handles. Just remember, any time you have deviation, you have to build more awareness. That's why if you choose a social media handle, keep it consistent across the board. Again, I know you love your name and want to use it, but if someone already has Brenda Smith , then you need to come up with something creative while still honoring your brand.

I'd recommend, at the very least, having your social media handles match on Twitter, Facebook, Instagram, LinkedIn, and YouTube. These are currently the major social media platforms. If you see a smaller, less-known social media platform on the list for NameCheck.com, then use your best judgment on whether you should or shouldn't open an account there.

Once you've unearthed a good fit, it's time to open and reserve the social media accounts. It will take a little time. Go to each platform and at least provide the necessary information and your author picture. If you don't have a professional headshot, then have someone shoot one for you and upload that as a placeholder. Once you get a professional headshot, you can go back through the platforms and upload it.

The most important part of setting up these social media profiles is brand congruency. Make sure your name is the same, the look is the same, and your message is the same. Make your message very clear where you have the opportunity. In some instances, like Twitter, you can do that in your description. It could be something as simple as:

Keep your Twitter profile clean and the images brand relevant.

You'll notice, I'm brief and don't go overboard. If you spend hours crafting long-form copy, the chances are likely your potential reader will not take the time to read it. Be precise about who you are, what you do, and what people can expect. Think of your description as an introduction to someone you just met. You don't want to make your first impression one where you're bloviating for hours at a time while your new-found acquaintance tunes you out. It's a simple conversation.

"What do you do, Dale?" asks my visitor.

"I'm an indie author, video content creator, and self-publishing advocate. What do you do?" I reply.

The most important step is to secure these social media profiles, not make them perfect. In due time, you'll change your profile image and refine your descriptions and bios. For now, just secure them, put in placeholders, and get ready for the next steps.

Just remember to keep brand congruency. When someone sees you on Instagram, they need to see the same thing on Twitter, Facebook, LinkedIn, YouTube, and beyond. That way, it's a familiar face, and there's no doubt that it's you who runs the profile.

Once you have your domain name and social media presence, you've done the basics. The whole point is you want to be easily accessible and discoverable online. This plays an important part not only in discovery but as an insurance policy. In the event Amazon kicks you off their platform, your readers will know where to find you. With a website and social media, your audience won't ever lose track of you.

Speaking of Amazon, let's get a look under the hood and find out how to best leverage the online juggernaut to build and grow your author platform. It's not going to be easy, but with a few simple steps and best practices, you'll be on your way to building an unstoppable author brand.

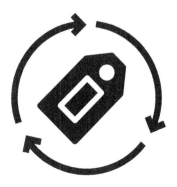

*E*veryone admires or loves a winner. There are few exceptions to this rule. When it comes to gaining the favor of a search engine algorithm, it's no different. Search engines function on a highly complex mathematical formula called an algorithm. How search queries get results is based in large part on:

- The overall customer experiences

- Previous browsing history

- Previous consuming behaviors

- Similar audience behaviors

Amazon's search engine algorithm is a fickle beast. Just when you think you gained its favor, it dumps you like a bad habit. One way you can coax the beast and win its love is through cold, hard, and consistent sales. How do you sell more books then? What do you need to do to sell books consistently?

At first, selling books is easy. After all, most everyone has a friend or family member willing to support the cause. However, once you burn through your inner circle contacts list, where do you go? Oddly enough, there's a much bigger world out there beyond your inner circle. All you have to do is be willing to step outside your comfort zone to welcome them in.

The bottom line, when it comes to gaining the favor of the Amazon algorithm, is to sell books. Because once you sell more books, Amazon will push your books to more customers who'll hopefully buy your books. Then, it becomes one beautifully rewarding cycle.

Amazon will push your book through a variety of avenues, including on their website through these options:

- Customers Also Bought

- Books You Might Like

- Frequently Bought Together

They'll also serve your book to their email subscribers and Kindle readers. There's no real way of guaranteeing Amazon will do this for you, and there's no set metric of how many sales you have to get before they start serving your book to other readers.

How Amazon Will NOT Build Your Audience for You

Amazon is in the business of selling products, not in the business of building other people's businesses. To be frank, Amazon is not your friend. They're merely a platform that fulfills customer orders. The online retailer is there for the customer and not you. It's a symbiotic relationship, though. If you were running a successful author brand through your site and Amazon chose to distribute or advertise through you, who would you honor more - your following or Amazon?

The answer is simple – your audience. Because your following is responsible for where you are and what you can do as an author, don't take it personally when Amazon doesn't prioritize your amazing epic novel about honey badgers and warlocks.

If Amazon sees some promise in your product, then they'll push it to the customers they see most fit for consuming it. If that audience doesn't buy, then you'll be at odds with the almighty algorithm. It's a sad reality. Amazon wants you to make sales. You must prove your worth before it even begins to get behind you.

Amazon will not build your audience for you. It's on you to do that. In the early days of Kindle Publishing, you could get away with finding a profitable keyword with low competition. Then, people would discover you easily, and you could run roughshod on the whole niche. Not anymore.

The Amazon Algorithm grows more sophisticated by the day, and the end goal of that algorithm is – customer satisfaction. Customers can't be satisfied if they search for a solution to their problems and go away empty-handed. That is a huge reason why I suggest authors to not rely on Amazon to push their book. You need to be the biggest cheerleader for your book because Amazon won't be until you've proven yourself.

That's why publishing and praying is not a reliable promotional strategy. Relying on outside forces to handle your marketing is a recipe for disaster. The few people who do succeed with this strategy are the unicorns of this business. Over 99% of authors need a solid approach to marketing, and it all starts with what you do off Amazon and before you launch your book.

All About Relevancy, Baby

In my book *Amazon Keywords for Books*, I discuss relevancy and how it works with search engines. The best way to establish relevance is through sales. Other factors play a role in building relevance for your

Title. After all, the more relevant your title is on Amazon, the more it'll serve your book to customers.

What if you're having no sales or minimal sales? How do you build relevance on your title? Beyond what I'm going to share in marketing and promotional strategies, you need to bear in mind one thing. Amazon loves new products, and it also loves products with refreshed data. If your book isn't faring so hot after thirty to ninety days, consider giving it a facelift.

A few ways you can breathe a little life back into your books is through the book cover. If you find your sales slumping, sometimes a new cover might be the trick to grab the attention of browsing customers. You might believe your book isn't appearing to customers. Believe it or not, Amazon does its part to place your product in front of potential buyers based on a few factors:

1. The customer's buying history

2. The customer's search history

3. Customers with similar buy & search history

4. Your book's keywords and category selection

With millions of customers visiting at any given moment on Amazon, I'm hard-pressed in thinking your book hasn't appeared in front of someone in some capacity. This is why an eye-catching, genre-specific cover is imperative to getting your ideal reader's attention. Get it wrong, and they'll scroll right past your book and never give it a second look. Get it right, and they'll at least visit your product page.

The next part is where your book could be failing to build relevancy – the book description. If you cannot give the browsing customer a compelling reason to buy your book, they'll most likely move onto other things. Sure, the Amazon algorithm likes when someone clicks on your book's product page link when brought up in a search query. Even better, the algorithm loves when a click leads to a sale.

How do you go from getting no sales to some sales? Improve your book's metadata, including:

1. Title, subtitle, series name

2. Book description

3. Seven backend keywords

4. Category placement

Update your metadata and allow Amazon to showcase your work to a different subset of customers. Once given the opportunity, you should hopefully see better results. If not, then you need to lean on more external factors. This means you don't go back and change your metadata again. Constantly changing your metadata confuses the algorithm and tosses your work into a mess of other confusing books.

The Publishing & Republishing Method

As mentioned previously, Amazon loves new products. It likes to test new products with its buyers to see if it'll take off and provide a larger bottom line. That's a huge reason why Amazon has a special subcategory for the bestseller's lists called Hot New Releases. This list consists of the bestselling print books and ebooks published in the last thirty days for a given category.

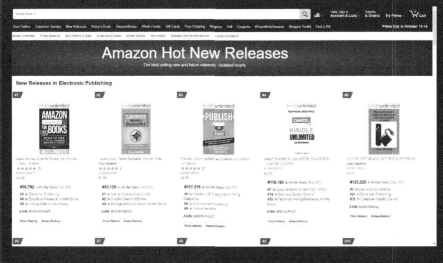

Amazon uses the Hot New Releases category to showcase the best performing books published in the last 30 days.

The Hot New Release bestseller list showcases what's performing best right now. It allows them to shine since already established books dominate the top of the bestseller's list for most categories. Otherwise, your book can't be heard above the noise and hit the top of the bestseller's lists. In a way, the Hot New Release lists level the playing field and provides an opportunity for newbies to shine. Think of it like open mic night, and you're finally getting your chance to sing for a willing audience.

What happens after the first thirty days is where it gets tricky. If you didn't prove your worth or take advantage of the spotlight, the Amazon algorithm is quick to discard your book and focus on the next shiny object and new release. You might notice the first thirty days to be beautiful while getting consistent sales beyond your wildest dreams. Then, day thirty-one comes, and your sales drop a little, followed by day thirty-two when you see even less. Day after day, week after week, your book drops in sales and sinks into obscurity.

At this point, you'll want to look into updating your book metadata. With ebooks, it's relatively simple to edit the title, subtitle, series name, and more. It's a bit more problematic when you want to update the same info on your print book since that information is static based on the ISBN (International Book Standard Number). That's okay because, in most instances, a slight adjustment in your book description and keyword choice could make all the difference.

I wouldn't recommend delisting your work and then republishing it. The problem is you erase all relevancy for that title and are starting over from scratch. Yes, inertia is a pain, but at least you have a proven commodity with some sales history. Once you delist that book and publish it anew, you're starting over and never really know what worked and what didn't.

Adjust the book metadata and wait. You must understand the effectiveness does not show in real-time. You can't change a book description and expect it to prove effective within twenty-four hours. Give your book time and breathing room. Allow the changes to take place at least thirty to ninety days before considering another change. It gives the algorithm time to know your product and test it in front of potential buyers.

Yes, the thirty-day window of a new release is nice! It's not the solution to a book that's not selling. The solution to a book not selling is creating a better book cover, crafting a better book description, and promoting the heck out of that book.

The Delisting & Republishing Scam to Avoid

About three or four years ago, a popular YouTube personality and go-to expert in self-publishing taught her coaching students to rely heavily

On the thirty-day window. If a book did well beyond the thirty-day window, then she'd have her students leave it alone. However, if sales dip at all beyond the first thirty days, she'd have them delist the title and republish it. The book was the same title with no deviation or change. In fact, it wasn't even a second edition.

The problem was two-fold:

1. Authors were gaming the system to get exposure instead of doing real marketing and promotion.

2. Customers thought the book was new despite it being a rerun.

This doesn't even address how some of these books had terrible reviews. Once the author delists the books, the bad reviews disappear, and the title reappears without a scratch. This is a bad business practice. If your title has low reviews, then you're doing something wrong. Merely delisting the title to remove bad reviews covers up your inadequacy to provide quality content readers want. Don't do this. If your book has low reviews, then the best thing to do is either delist the title and rewrite the entire thing or improve it and upload the updated version.

The latter option doesn't seem like fun, but you keep the history and relevance of the title. You also aren't duping the customers into buying your book despite having low reviews. Address the bad reviews by providing a better reading experience.

Thankfully, about two years ago, this self-publishing coach stopped teaching her students to game the system. She had them embrace better business practices like writing better content, executing sound promotional strategies, and building an author brand. Kudos to her!

Amazon Author Central — The Onsite Author Profile

Hey, even if you skipped my advice for getting a website and domain name, you've always got Amazon Author Central. While I lead you to believe Amazon isn't your friend, they are still committed to equipping you with the right tools to become successful. It's just up to you to use those tools to the best of their abilities. One of those tools is Amazon Author Central.

When you publish your book to the Amazon platform, the website indexes your content, including all the metadata. Indexing is the process of storing your product data, so it's discoverable through their search engine.

What if you could index your product beyond just the one time? Imagine being able to have your book more discoverable by listing it twice. That's not out of the realm of possibilities since Amazon Author Central is your solution.

An Amazon author profile is an excellent way for readers to see all your books in one spot.

Amazon Author Central is a way for authors to set up a profile related to their writing. The profile showcases your information on a customizable webpage with:

- An author bio

- An author picture

- All of the author's books

- Blog posts — You can link your blog but only do it if it's relevant to your niche. There's no sense in adding to the noise and cluttering up your page.

- Videos and pictures — do you have any promotional videos or graphics? Here's the spot to showcase it. If you made a book trailer, then your author profile is the spot to share it.

- A follow feature — visitors can follow a profile for notifications on new releases

Author Central also provides a suite of tools that help you optimize your book listing you can't otherwise do in your KDP dashboard. Think about all the missed opportunities you have when you only have seven backend keywords limited to fifty characters. That's okay! Now you can use Author Central for those missed keywords and discoverability.

This free option available to all authors with books published on Amazon (regardless of distribution management) has:

- Historical book sales rank tracking

- Additional metadata for all books including:

  > Editorial reviews

> Dustjacket metadata

> Miscellaneous information

- Regional sales tracking — this feature is nice if you want to know where you get a lot of sales to remarket & retarget buyers in a given region.

- And, more

Amazon Author Central is more than just a
place to set up your author profile.

Think of Author Central as a social media feature for Amazon. It allows readers another opportunity to see all your work showcased in one spot. It also allows you more customizable features on your product page, allowing you more opportunities for discovery.

Much like when you set up your social media profiles, you'll want to do the same with your author profile. Upload the same headshot you did for your social media profiles. Remember, brand congruency is mission-critical. People need to be able to spot your brand at a glance much in the same way someone sees the golden arches, and they think McDonald's. When someone sees the swoosh, they think Nike. Your headshot should be instant recognition. Engrain your pretty mug into people's minds to remember who you are as an author and brand.

Next, you'll want to create a short bio relevant to your niche. Far too often, I see struggling authors using this space to showcase their entire life. Don't do that. Only share information that is relevant to your niche. If you have a degree in exercise science and you're a fitness author, then certainly add that to your bio. However, if you're a science fiction fantasy writer, don't share it. Having a degree in exercise science has little to do with sci-fi fantasy.

When crafting your bio, don't worry about whether to write in first person or third person. The point is to write the best ad copy you can that paints an accurate picture of you. That way, random visitors and readers have a better insight into you as an author. Like a good book description, lead with a good opening hook. Then, craft short, punchy sentences readers can relate to. Keep your bio short to about 200-300 words. Anything longer is just extraneous.

Lastly, claim all your publications to post them on your profile. Once you claim your books, they'll all display neatly at the top of your page with the most popular publication on the left and the least popular on the right. Again, Amazon helps you out and showcasing what is most popular, so more buyers want to purchase your book.

Once you have everything set, Amazon will allow you to set a customized URL based on your author name. Choose what best fits, but don't get too hung up on it. Once you get a customized URL from Amazon, you can simply add a domain name, subdomain, or subdirectory to redirect to your Amazon profile.

For instance, to get to my author profile, I tell readers to visit DaleLRoberts.com/Amazon. This subdirectory redirects to the custom URL Author Central gave me of amazon.com/author/daleroberts. The custom URL is all well and good, but it's a bit harder to communicate and commit to memory than the URL redirect.

If you need further help with setting up your Amazon Author Central Profile, visit my video series at DaleLinks.com/AuthorCentral.

Remember how I had you reserve a domain name? Now it's time to put it to work. You need a safe space for your author brand. Think of it as your safe house in case anything goes sideways on any distribution platform. As a best practice, having a website gives you one spot to send all readers and visitors. Your website acts as a hub for all things involving your brand.

Did you have an interview recently? Great, showcase it on your website. Do you have a new release and want to announce it? Awesome! Showcase it on your website. Are you launching a podcast for your niche and unsure how to let people know? Excellent! Send people to your website.

Your website is the single most effective tool for your entire brand. If there's one area you should invest in, make it your website. It's where readers, brands, companies, and services can find you. As a bonus, it's an easy way to get people to remember your brand.

By now, you should have a general grasp of why you should get a domain name that's author specific. Let's discuss why you should invest just a little more and get site hosting. Can you get away with hosting your website through free services like Blogger, WordPress, or Wix? Sure! While you skirt the additional cost of hosting, you're greatly hindering your ability to be discovered through search engines.

Besides, nothing screams amateur hour like a website with another company's brand stamped all over it. Those services are free for a good reason – they get to promote your product and data mine your visitors. Yep, it's not a conspiracy theory. If you're driving traffic to your free website, you're doing it at the expense of your visiting audience. The service can remarket and retarget your audience without you having any say. The sad part is you're complicit because you didn't invest in premium site hosting.

I understand if you're cash-strapped and need a cost-effective solution. I highly recommend building in costs when launching your author brand for a domain name and site hosting. Between the two products, you can spend about $130 per year. That runs about $10.83 per month. If you sold about two books at a profit of $6, then you've already paid for it every month. You can sell two books per month, right? If not, continue reading, and you'll find out how.

When it comes to the right company to buy a domain name and site hosting, do your research. Ask around and see what most authors prefer. I don't want to lead you in one direction or the other. At the moment, I'm looking to move away from my current hosting service due to some complications (see here: DaleLinks.com/Hacked). I'll be the first to tell you websites are not my forte, and I wouldn't even know a TPS Report from a PHP. If you do enough research, you'll find a few features in common and the cost of the services.

Most website hosting packages run anywhere from $60 to $120 per year. Based on how much content you plan to put on your site, you may need to get a more expensive hosting package. Let's say you're an author with a background in photography. Chances are likely that you're going to need a bit more for your site to manage larger picture files.

Conversely, some fiction authors won't need much. If you're only show-casing front cover images and author signings, then you only need a basic site hosting package, nothing too elaborate. Either way, if you're unfamiliar, I'd recommend starting at the most basic website hosting package, and you can always upgrade when you need it.

Plan an expense every year for your website hosting and domain name. Many authors forget about these expenses. When it comes time to pay the bill, they become delinquent or shut down their site. That's a horrible situation, especially if you pick up enough authority and search engines index your content. You leave your domain name open to bad actors who'll buy up your property. Then, when you need it, they'll sell it to you at a higher premium. Don't let it escalate to that point.

Having a website isn't essential, but it is necessary to build a lasting presence online without the aid of social media and retail platforms. Ultimately, your website is your safe space. If social media shuts you down or puts you off, you can always send your readers and followers to your website. If an online retail platform decides for whatever reason they've had enough of your books and kicks you off, then readers will know precisely where to find you.

Too many authors romanticize the business of self-publishing through platforms like Amazon or its competitors. They believe this train will go on forever. And, for most, it will. For a select few, Amazon has the sole discretion to kick them off. They do not need a reason to do so. It's their sandbox, and we're merely playing in it.

Last year, a friend mentioned how a mutual acquaintance fell on hard times. In the previous years, this author was building a six-figure per month romance publishing business. He had all his eggs in the Amazon basket. Though he allegedly was doing everything by the book, Amazon terminated his account. He didn't have a website. He didn't even have a mailing list. This author had nothing and nowhere for his readers to know where to begin to find him.

Imagine making over $100,000 per month in revenue and not pulling out an insurance policy as a safeguard for worst-case scenarios. If this author had only put together an email list, he could send subscribers to his website. With six-figures in revenue, he had the readers. He could rely entirely on his website to fulfill orders. Yet he naively relied on Amazon to be there for him forever.

Don't rely on Amazon for everything, folks. The reality is Amazon isn't your friend. They're merely a platform you can leverage to build your author platform. Conversely, you are also a tool they use to get more sales. When you understand publishing on Amazon is merely a transactional relationship, you'll take better steps to safeguard your business. One of those first steps is to set up your author website today!

Amazon Associates – Getting Paid for Selling Your Books

You might be a little confused seeing a section about getting paid for selling your books in a chapter about marketing through your website. Stick with me on this one, because it requires a deeper explanation. You're already getting paid to sell your books, so what's the big deal with Amazon Associates?

A few years ago, I'd stumbled on some fine print on Amazon Author Central. In the Author Central dashboard, you'll see recommendations for making the most of your product listing on Amazon. In one single line, you might notice Author Central recommends something called Amazon Associates.

Amazon Associates is an affiliate marketing platform where Amazon pays you to advertise their products. What is affiliate marketing, you might ask? Affiliate marketing is where a company or service will pay you for referring people to them. Sometimes you will be paid for simply referring new customers, and most of the time, you will be paid for referring paid customers.

Here's how affiliate marketing works. I watched and enjoyed the latest movie with Dwayne "The Rock" Johnson. When I finished watching it, I told my friends they should go check it out. Under normal circumstances, I get nothing out of the referral. I only get the satisfaction of sharing a good movie-going experience with a friend.

Imagine getting paid for sending your friends to watch The Rock's latest movie. What if you got paid for sending people to that theater even if they didn't end up watching The Rock's movie? Affiliate marketing works in the same way.

If you like a service, product, or company, you can align yourself with that company through an affiliate program. Any time you send traffic or paying customers, you get a small percentage of the sale. The best part is the referred customers don't pay any more for the services than they normally would while you get a small kickback. Pretty neat, right?

The Amazon Associates program works in the same way; however, what the customer buys will dictate how much you get paid.

"Wait, Dale. Didn't you say I'd get paid more for selling my books?"

I'm glad you asked because you get paid in two of three ways.

1. You get paid a royalty for the sale of the book through KDP.

1. You get paid a percentage of the sale price on Amazon (typically 4%).

2. You get paid for any other sales made on the platform 24 hours after the customer uses your referral link.

The last part is one that blows everyone's minds. First, referring traffic to your book is a given. If you aren't sending traffic and potential readers to your book on Amazon, then we need to fix that right now. Next, you get paid a percentage of the sale price. That percentage is like Amazon giving you a cut of their take just for being a good sport and sending customers. Last, even if a customer doesn't buy your book, but they buy a product on Amazon, you get compensation.

Wild, right? Let's say you send people to buy your book. The customer doesn't buy your book but gets other items. When they make that purchase, you get a small commission. In a best-case scenario, the referred customer buys your book and products, thereby increasing your affiliate earnings.

How do you get an Amazon Associates account? It's not easy, but it's simple. You'll need…wait for it…a website! Ding ding ding! Hence why I inserted this subchapter about Amazon Associates in the chapter about building a website.

Visit affiliate-program.amazon.com to apply for an account. It's a rather lengthy process but somewhat intuitive. Though you get instant access to creating affiliate links, you should hold off. Wait to set up an Amazon Associates account until you have one thing dialed in – your website.

Amazon wants you to be their little worker bee and drive as many microtransactions as possible. The more worker bees they have out there, the more money you both earn. Amazon is a publicly-traded company and doesn't just want anyone sending traffic. They have specific standards they like to adhere to. Rather than go through their entire terms of services, guidelines, and policies, I'll give you the important, need to know facts.

One of the main requirements Amazon has is affiliates need to have a website or online presence to drive traffic. They want proof of concept. Having any old micro-website won't do. Amazon wants you to advertise their product, but not have that be the only thing you do. After all, they're doing a damned good job at advertising their website. Why do they need another website that does the same? You're not different.

That's why it's paramount you build out your website with content. Fill your website with relevant content about you. Here are a few suggestions to include in your website to increase your chances of entering and staying in the Amazon Associates program:

1. **Welcome Page** — This is simply your website's main landing page. You should have your author name, a picture of you, and/or your latest book. Then let them know what they can expect on your website.

2. **About Page** — Showcase who you are through a professional headshot and well-written author bio. You may want to include contact information or relevant social media links.

3. **Contact Page** — Set up a simple contact form, so you don't have your email out there for spammers and hackers to get. Most web forms are free and integrate well with website hosting services.

4. **Blog** — You're an author, so act like one! I'm not telling you to write blog posts every day in perpetuity. Simply create about six to twelve different posts trickled out over about two to four

1. weeks. First, the blog posts aid in discoverability on Google and other search engines. Next, you showcase your writing skills and can promote your backlog of books. Lastly, you have content for people to consume that isn't just a bunch of affiliate links.

2. **Bookshelf** — This is simply a recommendation and not a necessity. This webpage showcases all your publications with Amazon product page links. Since you went through the trouble of creating an author website and writing a book, you might as well showcase your work. The best part is you can later use your bookshelf to insert your Amazon Associates links.

Need to Know Info about Amazon Associates

Once you get a website set up like previously mentioned and you've applied for your account, wait for approval from Amazon Associates. They'll typically email you within one to two weeks after applying. If you don't hear back right away, be patient.

A while ago, I was working on a side project with a close friend. With a customized domain name on a simple website, we set up an Amazon Associates account. Rather than wait for the approval, we created links through Amazon and posted them to our website. We were getting sales, and our Amazon Associates dashboard showed a nice return.

Within a week or two, we received the bad news. Amazon rejected our application based on the lack of available content on our website. We essentially didn't have enough meat on the bones for our website. Again, Amazon doesn't want your site to be solely their website links. They want you to be an actual legit website devoted to other things beyond selling Amazon's wares.

Equipped with this information, my friend and I got quickly to work and created about twelve blog posts we fired off daily for two weeks. It was enough content to prove we were more than an Amazon link dumping ground. We reapplied, waited two weeks, and Amazon sent an approval email.

What You Should & Shouldn't Do

The most critical step many affiliate marketers make is in fully disclosing the nature of the links. You can't simply rely on people to know what affiliate links are. You need to tell people in a public space on your website the nature of your relationship with Amazon, what the links lead to, and how it compensates you for sharing it. Sadly, this isn't so much an Amazon rule, but more a Federal Trades Commission (FTC) rule.

Since you're sending visitors to another site where you get paid for them visiting or buying something, you must tell your visitors that. You can simply do it in the post showcasing the link, or create a separate page with the disclosure. If you're doing the latter option, use a link to direct visitors for the full disclosure. Doing both will not hurt, and I even recommend it, so you aren't caught off guard.

Some people believe since you're getting paid for referring traffic that it influences your decision to promote a given product or service. In this case, it affects your decision. You're sending traffic to buy your book. You're getting paid more for it! Why wouldn't you be inclined to send people?! Just simply state something like:

> Full disclosure: The outbound link is part of an affiliate program where I'm compensated for any sales. This does not change the pricing for customers and greatly helps support this website.

Don't go overboard, and don't sweat it if anyone tries to call you on being a shill for Amazon. If you're going to have your book on Amazon, you might as well get paid for it. And, if you're going to promote your book on Amazon, you might as well get paid even more for it. After all, most customers aren't simply going to stop after buying your book. You sent a warm buyer into Amazon's hands. So, you might as well reap the rewards for sending the traffic and all the previous work of writing and publishing your book.

Creating a link can be somewhat confusing at first. You don't just want to sign up for Amazon Associates and then copy the URL in the browser. That's something you can do without Amazon Associates. With the program, you'll want to enable SiteStripe for Amazon Associates. Once enabled, visit Amazon.com and search for your book. Find your book, go to its product page. Then, click **Text** below **Get link** in the top left corner of SiteStripe. A pop-up window will show a highlighted short link—press **CTRL** and the letter **C** to copy it.

SiteStripe is the gray strip at the top of the Amazon browser when you're signed in as an Amazon Associate.

Then, go to where you wish to share the link—press **CTRL** and the letter **V** to paste it where you want. Now, when someone clicks that link, they'll be sent to Amazon and will be earmarked as your referred customer. This marking doesn't last forever and has a limited reach (about twenty-four hours). But, during that time, if a customer comes back and orders a product through Amazon, you get credit for it. That's regardless of it being your book or not.

Now, don't make the same mistake I did for my first few years of using Amazon Associates. According to their guidelines, you must use the exact link given to you. You cannot create a subdirectory, subdomain, or link shorteners (i.e., bitly, etc.) to redirect customers to Amazon. Though you might think how you send traffic isn't a big deal, some bad actors find nefarious ways to game the system. Rather than getting lumped in with that lot, stick to the rules.

That's probably one of the main reasons why Amazon doesn't want their links covered. Ever since learning I could not create domain redirects, I've done my best to correct course and strictly use Amazon's short links. The nice part about using Amazon short links is most people can tell it's an Amazon link. That's instant credibility and assurance the customer isn't visiting a sketchy website.

SiteStripe also has two social media buttons integrated into the dash. If you want to share your link via Facebook or Twitter, all you have to do is click the button, and you'll be whisked away to the respective platform. Then, customize your message and post it.

The biggest takeaway when it comes to using Amazon Associates is to be obvious. Share the link as it is and disclose the nature of the link. Don't go overboard with your links and beat people up 24/7 with it. Use it tastefully, and you'll see big returns with consistent efforts over the long haul.

Additional features in the Amazon Associates program make the program all the more rewarding but be selective. For instance, bounty programs give you more money for referrals. Amazon sets up special bonus rewards every few months for specific product types. If you're new to Amazon Associates, I'd recommend keeping it simple. Don't spread yourself too thin with all the features.

Ad embedding is one advertising feature Amazon offers. Having the ability to embed Amazon ads is nice, but you have to ask yourself, "What would my visitor think?" Is your website visitor supposed to focus on you or focus on buying products on another site?

Embedding Amazon widgets is nice, but I don't recommend it for a few reasons:

1. It distracts from your brand and sends visitors off your website. Most widgets display products that are not your books. Do you want to sell more books or sell other people's products?

2. The embedded widgets can slow down your website load time. Some visitors don't like waiting an extra three seconds while your Amazon widget populates on the page.

3. Having ads all over your website can make your website appear cluttered like a disorganized yard sale.

For me, I do not like putting the Amazon widget on my website. I did it for a hot minute on my fitness website, but then I started thinking about the visitor's first impression. Do I want first-time visitors to remember Amazon or me? I'll take the latter over the former. No one needs help remembering Amazon. Take every advantage you can get when it comes to your website.

Remember, with your website, less is more. This isn't just regarding Amazon widgets; it also includes your books and product recommendations. If you're going to use the Amazon Associates links, choose one page for all your relevant links. This is where a virtual bookshelf comes in handy. If you must include affiliate links on any pages of your bookshelf, limit how many you use to about one to two. Using too many affiliate links across your entire site can work against you.

This isn't so much to make a cleaner visiting experience. It's also due in large part to significant changes in the Google search engine algorithm. Google wants to send you traffic, but it will only trust websites it knows visitors will enjoy and consume. The name of the game on Google is data mining. If Google sends a customer to your website and the customer leaves, Google is less apt to send more customers. With a shorter customer experience on your website, Google has less data about that customer who used their search engine.

Conversely, when a customer visits your website and stays on your website longer, then Google deems your site to have more relevance based on your given topic. Having many affiliate links can be off-putting to visitors and create a disjointed customer journey that's hard for Google to track. Many industry experts state having too many affiliate links all over your site can be detrimental to long-term website discoverability and relevance.

The lesson is don't go buck wild on your affiliate links. You don't want your author platform to take a backseat to your affiliate marketing efforts. Select your affiliate links wisely, post them on one page, and if you must share any links outside your main affiliate link page, keep it to one to two links.

Lastly, avoid sharing Amazon Associates links in your email marketing efforts. Some email marketing platforms forbid any affiliate links in email broadcasts. Be careful about what you share in your email campaigns. We'll briefly touch on email marketing later in the book. Just remember the primary purpose of email marketing is to build a relationship with your subscriber. You can't build a good long-term relationship if all you do is assault the subscriber with nothing but affiliate links.

Simply leverage email marketing as a way to deliver traffic to your website. From there, let your website do all the heavy lifting. On your site, you can share your Amazon associates link or any other affiliate link. Besides, you give your email subscriber the option to view your offer or not. Giving your customer the higher ground builds more trust in the long run.

*L*et's get one thing straight. When it comes to social media marketing and promotion, I'm not the foremost expert. I know enough to make me dangerous. To be honest, no single methodology will be right or wrong. Telling you exactly how you should conduct yourself on social media is like trying to mold you into another version of me. You need to find your way and discover your voice.

One thing is for certain, social media is here to stay and has become an integral part of most everyone's lives. Can you avoid marketing and promotion through social media? Sure. Should you? No. I can see how you'd feel that way. Some people see an ocean of opportunity and get overwhelmed, while others might have had a bad experience and swore off all social media.

The fact is, quite a few of your potential readers and customers are residing on social media. If you want to get your ideal readers' attention, you need to meet them where they are. Not all readers are just hanging out on Amazon in the reviews section or forum. Quite a few of them congregate on Twitter, Facebook Groups, YouTube channels, and beyond.

Before you attack any social media marketing, you need to know your ideal reader. As covered in the previous book, *Amazon Keywords for Books*, if you try to write for everyone, you write for no one in the process. Marketing and promotion work much in the same way. If you're marketing and promoting to everyone, then you're marketing and promoting to no one.

Social media is much like a crowded bus transporting its customers from one place to the next. The bus is jammed full of people carrying a variety of conversations at a fever pitch volume. If you come onto that bus screaming about your latest book, no one is going to listen. You're simply that crazy person who got on the bus at the last stop and is trying to bum a smoke for later on. No one will make eye contact with you, and no one wants to share a seat with you.

What you need to do is find a familiar face and a group of people you can relate to. Think of them as your tribe. Once you identify commonalities in your tribe or community, you can better assimilate with the rest of them. Get comfortable and get to know people. Don't worry about selling your latest book. The most important part about leveraging social media for selling more books is to build the relationship first. Human beings buy from other human beings. Until you can build a sense of know, like, and trust with your ideal audience, nothing you say will ever matter.

John C. Maxwell once stated:

People don't care what you know until they know that you care.

Get good at getting to know people and truly put meaning behind your interactions. Don't sweat the sales; they'll come in due time.

Once you know who your ideal reader is, identify the social media platform they most frequently visit. Sadly, no part of this book will tell you where to find your werebear shapeshifter romance readers – whether in Facebook Groups or on Reddit. This is where you're going to have to study where other readers are congregating. From there, you'll need to ask yourself:

1. Can I see myself using this social media platform consistently?

2. Will I devote myself to learning this social media space?

3. Can I put my book sales on the back burner while I build real relationships?

Once you can identify the platform you wish to work on, it's time to stake your claim and place your flag in the sand. Even though I told you to go easy on beating up people about your author brand, I don't want you to think you should be a wolf in sheep's skin. The best way to be forward about who you are and what you're about is to show it. Where do you start, and what do you need?

What You Absolutely Need on Social Media

Earlier in the book, I had you reserve all the social media handles on every platform. Remember, don't sweat using every platform right now. I'm just going to get you to use one. For now, you're going to need brand congruency. The first part of being consistent is your name, your profile picture, and your profile information. When people visit you on the various platforms, they need to know it's you and not some impostor. The best way to mitigate those issues is by getting your brand matching across every platform. Don't become overwhelmed at having all these profiles. It's not your mission to manage all of them. Just pick one for now and go with it. If you build enough presence on one platform, then you can spread out to another one in due time. For instance, I didn't focus on building much, if any presence, beyond YouTube when I first started my channel, *Self-Publishing with Dale*. My attention was solely on growing my brand there. Though I had some presence on other platforms, I was only concerned about increasing my reach on YouTube. Once I broke about 1,000 active subscribers, I started looking into other avenues without distracting me from my mission of growing on YouTube.

Take your time to grow your presence. Be patient, and don't worry if the results don't come right away. It takes time, patience, and a bit of perseverance to win in the long game. Do not expect to start selling books like a maniac just because you've been camping out in a Facebook Group every minute for the past three months. It will take a lot more engagement and interaction before people start to trust you and bring you into their inner circle.

Much like any social interaction, your approach is the perceptions others will have of you. I often think about this kid, Simon, who was in a Facebook Group of other self-publishers. Simon was a bull in a China shop. He was very opinionated, lacked any real filter, and always seemed on the verge of selling something new he discovered online.

On the opposite end of the spectrum was Ava. She was the head moderator of the same group. Though she chimed in for quite a few conversations, she always delivered excellent insights and never seemed to have an ulterior motive. Ava was simply there to put the socializing in social media. Through a conversation with a client, I'd come to find out Ava did virtual assistant work. Instantly, I remembered all her contributions to this Facebook Group and how she was incredibly giving of herself. There was instant trust in what she had to offer as a freelance assistant.

I never imagined I'd be working with her for over four years! I've driven tons of referrals and new clients her way, and her business exploded.

Now, think if my client had referred me to Simon. How would that conversation have gone? Most likely, I'd be dismissive and pass at working with him. Why? Because I'd remember how he conducted himself. He was always taking and never giving.

You, as an author, must remember every interaction on social media will have rippling effects on your career for years to come. Before you get into a spit fight, before you shill your latest affiliate product, before you beat people up with links to your website, remember to be an Ava, not a Simon.

Social Media Etiquette 101

In the early days of social media, quite a few methods worked to bolster followers and grow an online presence. Fortunately, those days have long since gone. Yet many people still believe some outdated methods work for blowing up on social media. Don't waste your time on these outdated tactics for growing your social media presence.

Follow for Follow

Gone are the days when you could use your number of social media followers to flex your clout. Is a social media following important? Yes, but does it make any difference if those followers are inactive? Absolutely! Having an arbitrary number of followers is defeating the purpose. You want to have active followers who engage in your content and posts.

One of the worst, most ineffective ways to grow on any social media platform is Follow for Follow. It's a simple quid pro quo system. Two people on social media follow each other to help fluff their numbers. The tactic would be good if only it were a legitimate relationship.

Otherwise, it's simply followers with no real engagement. The key to success in social media is engagement. Modern-day currency comes by way of engagement. If you don't see any engagement on social media, then you're spinning your wheels.

It can happen to the best of us. We see other people crushing it on Instagram, YouTube, Twitter, and more. Their follower number seems to be the key to their success. Frankly, it's much more than the number of people following them. It's all about the attention they get on their given platform. No exception!

Don't bother following someone if you don't legitimately know, like, or trust the person. You can and should expect the same of people surrounding you. No one owes you a thing on social media. You don't deserve to have a certain number of followers. Until you can prove your merit and get real engagement, you won't get real followers.

Real followers are what is going to work, so don't bother doing follow for follow tactics. Don't fall into the trappings of group followings. Follow who you like, and others will follow you if it makes sense to them.

Zero Spamming Zone

> Spam (verb) — to send irrelevant or inappropriate messages to a large number of people.

Imagine taking someone out for a date. You have the whole evening planned out, you got dressed up for the occasion, and even put on your best smell good spray. Once you pick up your date, you simply jump to the part you like best – making out! Yep, you dive in hard for that big ol' kiss despite only just meeting this person.

Can you imagine the reaction of your date? You'll probably get a weird look at a minimum. Or worse yet, you might get a violent reaction.

When it comes to life in general:

> No one likes someone selling to them.

Everyone likes to feel in control of most aspects of life. We want to buy things on our terms. When we're hungry, we go to the store. When we need gas for our cars, we go to the gas station. When we take a lei-surely stroll through the mall, we immediately get into defensive mode when the mall kiosk worker assaults us with their sea salts, lotions, or perfumes. Why? We weren't looking for sea salts, lotions, or perfumes, and this person has entered into our space and commanded our time and attention without permission.

Now, this isn't a punch down on mall kiosk salespeople. It's more to demonstrate how people don't like to be sold anything without prior consent or knowledge. That's why you should never go into social media with the expectations to sell books hand over fist. Outside of running paid ads through Facebook, Twitter, or more, selling your wares can be off-putting to the random person who doesn't know you on social media.

If you're going to share your book, great, but you must have context first and a reason to do it beyond getting more book sales. Additionally, you'll want to make sure it's an okay practice based on the platform. I know on Reddit, most people detest self-promotion, and it sometimes results in termination from their communities called Subreddits. You need to read the room first before ever selling anything.

Even though it might seem okay, ask yourself:

1. If I saw this post from someone I don't know, would I find it helpful?

    A. If not, don't post it.

    B. If so, prove it by posting it. Then, see what type of engagement you get.

2. Will this erode the trust people have in me?

    A. If so, then don't post it.

    B. If not, then ask a few peers their opinion about it.

Spamming seems to be the easy answer, especially if you're playing a numbers game. Maybe, just maybe, you can entice one out of every one-hundred people to buy your book. All you had to do was quickly post an offer for your book in fifty Facebook Groups. If you post in fifty groups and have a hundred people in each group who see your post, you'll have fifty people interested in checking out your book on Amazon. How likely do you think that all fifty will buy? To believe you will convert one hundred percent of your visitors is insane! Let's say you have at least one out of ten people who'll buy. Then, that means in a best-case scenario, you're looking at five people buying your book.

All the while, you made this ridiculous scene in front of hundreds of people. The other 4,995 people are privy to your ways and are more apt to tune you out the next time you spam them with your latest offer. Even worse still, you might have people who'll see your work later and pass based on their first impression of your author brand.

With spamming, just don't do it. It's a waste of valuable time, energy, and effort for everyone, including you.

Tagging People — Relevant vs. Irrelevant

This doesn't apply across all platforms, but a vast majority have a feature where you can tag other people. The process of tagging is where you link another person to your post, so their following sees your post too. In theory, tagging another person makes sense, especially if it drives more engagement. Is tagging relevant to the post, or are you simply thirsty for attention from other people and riding the coattails of someone else's hard work?

I cannot begin to tell the number of times I have had to block someone on Twitter who tags me with irrelevant tweets. Inevitably, when I visit the person's profile, I find they have few followers and focus only on selling their service. This is a one-way ticket to the block button. I don't have time for people who want to leech off the attention given to me through my hard work to drive traffic to their platform.

Worse yet is when someone tags without any prior consent, context, or reason beyond pushing their agenda. No one minds a tag if it makes sense! Much like sales, no one likes to go into that transaction without permission.

When you want to increase the relevancy of a social media post, then, by all means, invite other people to the conversation through tagging. Make sure:

- It's okay with the tagged person
- There's context
- You have an end goal in mind

I've written this many times before, and I'll write it many times after. Deliver value first and be a human being. Everything else will fall into place after that. If tagging seems fit for the conversation, then by all means, do it. Don't merely tag someone for the sake of bolstering your reach. Do it because it's going to help people.

Post Frequency

How often should you post, and does it matter? When it comes to how frequent you should post, you need to measure the effectiveness, reach, and engagement of your posts first before you ratchet up the number of times you do it. For instance, on YouTube, many experts used to spout how daily video posts were how you succeeded. After all, Pewdiepie, one of the world's most-followed YouTubers, grew his social following by posting every day for ten years. Pewdiepie is different than you and carved out a niche for himself.

Look on the other end of the spectrum with YouTuber Mark Rober. He merely posts once per month and gets millions of views, watch time minutes, and social engagement. Even though Mark doesn't post every day, he makes his monthly posts power-packed and effective.

Before you commit to posting on your preferred social media platform, study the landscape, and take note of the successful influencers:

1. What are they doing?

2. How often are they posting?

3. How is their engagement?

Can you model your post frequency based on the successful influencers? What can you do to tweak it and make it yours? You don't need to be the next Pewdiepie or Mark Rober. Just be yourself and adjust as you go according to what resonates most with your audience.

Social Media Examples

I've tried to keep this book as evergreen as possible. However, I'm sure some aspects will not remain evergreen forever, especially as popularity rises or falls based on the trending platform. Despite the dangers of sharing less evergreen content, I'm going to do it anyway because it's the concepts you need to embrace, not the exact platform.

Facebook: Ads, Groups, Business Pages, Oh My!

Over the past few years, Facebook seems to have undergone a massive public punch down. Many people would have you believe Facebook is for stuffy, old curmudgeons shouting about politics and religion. The numbers tell a different story! Billions of users use the Facebook platform daily,[10] so this doesn't equate. It reminds me of how millions of music lovers throw shade on Nickelback. Yet, the band still manages to sell millions of records, sell-out stadiums, and grow in popularity. What gives?

Facebook may not be for everyone, but one could say the same for almost all social media platforms. Billions of consumers use Facebook, so leveraging this platform is a no-brainer for authors.

The options are overwhelming at first between running ads, business pages, and groups. Where do you start, and what is most important? Many would-be experts want you to believe organic growth is dead on Facebook, but I've found that to be a half-truth.

Years ago, you could set up a Facebook business page as an author, drive a bunch of likes to the page, and reach tens of thousands of readers.

Once Facebook saw they were missing out on the money-making opportunity, they tweaked their algorithm to suppress the organic reach of Facebook Business pages. This required authors to dig deep into their pockets and run ads to build relevancy on the platform.

Sure, Facebook ads can be a viable option for growing your author brand. Still, for most indie authors, it's not an affordable and sustainable option. Once you stop spending, it's not like Facebook is going to keep delivering traffic. They shut that facet off and turn their backs to you.

What if you could still get organic reach on Facebook? What if you could reach more readers organically? It's 100% possible, but it's going to require a little upfront work.

First, you needed to start a Facebook Group yesterday. Right now, Facebook Groups are the single most effective way to market directly to your ideal readers and audience. Facebook doesn't require running ads on your posts to build awareness. If you want help in getting your Facebook Group started and growing, watch my video series on YouTube at DaleLinks.com/FacebookGroups.

Next, build awareness about your business page. Whether you do it through a post on your profile or share it in your latest book, people need to know it's there. Then, you'll have to educate your audience on the best practices. If someone is interested enough in following you, they will take the right measures to see your posts.

You could simply tell your potential followers:

> Like and follow my author page at
> Facebook.com/SelfPubWithDale. Then turn the Follow
> Settings to See First, so you don't miss out on any free
> promotions, advanced reader copies, and special deals.

Tell your reader what's in it for them and exactly what they need to do. Otherwise, they won't bother with it. You will find if you abbreviate your request and keep it as simple as possible, you'll get more results. Once you fire off a post, you're more apt to get people to see it if they're following your business profile. The tricky part is getting engagement. Without engagement, your organic reach is nil. Never fear! There are a few ways you can tip engagement in your favor:

- Create posts in bite-sized chunks. Avoid long paragraphs. Instead, break up your sentences into separate lines.

- Use emojis to grab attention. It seems silly and somewhat childish, but it's fast becoming the way to command attention on a busy platform.

- Use imagery either through a picture, GIF, or video. You get bonus points if you add captions to your video. Skip to the resources section for my recommendation for quality captioning.

- Lead with a hook. You need to command attention and only have five to six words to do it, so lead with your best stuff. Think of it as the headline of a newspaper.

- Finish with a compelling question visitors can't resist. People love to share their thoughts, so if you ask them a question or to share their thoughts, they'll most likely do that.

- Always get the last word. To make the most of your engagement, you need to respond to all comments and close with an open-ended question. This keeps the conversation going while sending signals to Facebook's algorithm about the relevance of your post.

Organic reach on Facebook isn't dead. It just requires more work. Quite a few people don't want to put in the work, or they want to throw money at the problem. If you have the discretionary expense, then go for it! However, if you don't and won't bother with it, don't be surprised if you get no engagement and no growth on this lucrative platform.

One feature you can use on a Facebook Business Page is a shop. That is a great place to showcase your catalog of books. Be sure to link out the appropriate areas on Amazon. That isn't an avenue I've fully explored myself, but it's an option worth considering.

Twitter

Do not sleep on Twitter. I discovered how much I left on the table over the past few years since taking Twitter much more seriously. Rewind to between 2014 and 2015. Twitter seemed like a link dumping ground for me. Frankly, I didn't understand all the hashtags, random conversations, and trending topics. One thing I knew for sure was authors and entrepreneurs were crushing it there. I felt, at a bare minimum, I needed to get on the platform even if to add to the white noise.

As traction grew on Twitter, I started gaining the attention of various podcasters, influencers, and businesses. I landed interviews, collaborations, and sponsorships through the platform. My network exploded tenfold due to simply being active about fifteen to twenty minutes per day.

On the platform that limits you to 280 characters, doesn't let you edit a Tweet, and is the stomping grounds for the Cancel Culture Elite, you can strike out if you aren't careful. How do you leverage this platform? What are the best practices? Is this going to yield immediate results?

The best way to leverage Twitter is simply by starting. At first, you're going to be posting tweets to an audience of no one. The first thing you need to do is find and follow anyone you know on Twitter. Scroll and engage in posts of interest to you and are relevant to your niche.

Next, browse all trending topics and hashtags. You may even have to guess your way through hashtags to see if you can find your ideal audience. Though it may seem humbling and exhausting at first, if you put just a little effort in every day on Twitter, it'll pay off in the long term.

When I'm dry on ideas about what to share, I simply find someone else's tweet, then retweet it with a comment. Post your thoughts about the tweet, throw on about two to three relevant hashtags, and fire it off.

Also, you should already have a relevant profile pic and banner art. The next thing you'll need is a pinned tweet. This is an excellent time to showcase your latest book, website, or anything that'll draw more eyes to your brand. You can simply post about your latest book and leave it alone. The nice thing about pinned tweets is you can leave it up indefinitely. As readers trickle into your Twitter profile, they'll have a reminder of who you are and what you do.

Similar to the Facebook posts, you'll want to have your tweet include a few eye-catching and search engine optimized elements:

- Lead with a hook to grab attention.

- Include those cute little emojis. Again, I know it seems silly, but it's becoming ingrained in popular culture. Those who embrace

- it will get attention while the rest gamble with dropping into obscurity.

- Make sure you have an image, GIF, or video. If you're promoting your book, then that's probably going to be the most fitting image. I included recommendations of free or premium image services for your book in the resources section later in the book.

Tag relevant Twitter profiles when there's context. If I have a conversation with my buddy @KWheelerBooks and I share it via Twitter, then I'm going to tag him. However, do not tag someone simply to leverage their audience to build yours. It's off-putting and, in some instances, will get you blocked by that person. I've had the displeasure of being tagged without any prior permission or context. Be selective about who you tag and why you're tagging them.

If it's a close friend, then all bets are off. Just don't go overboard like some crazed and desperate MLM salesperson trying to promote their latest income opportunity or disgusting nutritional shake. You'll turn off more people than turn them on.

Quite a few people want to know the frequency of posts. This largely depends on the time you can afford. I've known some people to tweet every hour on the hour. While some only do it once per day. If you're planning to tweet frequently, you may want to consider using an automated social media posting service. From Hootsuite to ContentStudio, you've got quite a few free and premium services to help manage social media posting without you having to camp out waiting for the right time to tweet out.

Instagram

Admittedly, I was late to the game on Instagram. This platform out-wardly appears to be nothing but a collection of highly photogenic models and inspirational quotes. There's far more to Instagram than you'd think. Since it directly integrates with Facebook, it should be an avenue for you to consider if you're already on Facebook.

If you're going to break ground on this platform, here are the things you need to know:

1. You need an eye-catching image or video. Do not go with grainy, potato-quality pictures from a 1990's flip phone. It just doesn't cut the mustard.

2. Long-form video resides on their IGTV feature. If you happen to shoot a book trailer or promotional video longer than one minute, you can always add it to IGTV. The nice part is you can still showcase the first minute of content on your Instagram wall.

3. Create short or long-form text that tells a story. The point of the comment is to add context to the picture. Lead with a hook, break up paragraphs into single lines, and toss in some emojis where you see fit.

4. Hashtags are a must if you want others to discover you. You can use up to thirty hashtags on a single post. Some people believe you won't get as much organic traffic if you put hashtags in the post, so they put them in the first comment instead. I don't sweat the small stuff and just add the hashtags at the end of the text.

The key to crushing it on Instagram and getting your book exposed is through building relationships. Once it's time to promote your book or post something relevant about your book in your stories, people will take notice. Take your time. Explore relevant hashtags, follow people in your niche, and comment on posts with no intention of putting the spotlight on you.

Do not leave disingenuous comments and finish with "check out my profile" or "hey, I've got a book you should buy."

Nothing screams desperation like taking the spotlight from the original poster. If you want to do everyone a favor, drop a genuine comment, and then share the picture to your stories feature. Don't forget to tag the original poster, so they know you like their content.

LinkedIn

Gone are the days of dropping your resume and calling it a day on LinkedIn. This is no longer the stuffy business professional's social media platform. Since Microsoft acquired LinkedIn around 2016, they modeled other popular social media platforms with big-time success.

LinkedIn is great for establishing yourself as the go-to authority in your niche. You can connect with your peers and other business professionals, share your latest book, and drop some 4-1-1 on related topics.

My good friend and indie author, Professor Nez, staked his claim many years ago and stood by LinkedIn for the longest time. As the site underwent major changes, Nez won big time! Because he remained so active for so many years, he has tens of thousands of followers, and his posts get plenty of eyeballs. Nez was fortunate enough to leverage his exposure on LinkedIn to land five-figure speaking gigs based on his forte in career consultation.

Imagine that – getting paid $10,000 to speak about what you love most, just by being active on a social media platform. Well, it's entirely possible, and it's even more lucrative if you're a nonfiction author. Since LinkedIn functions as a business to business social media platform, naturally, you've got a solution to their problem.

The more active and visible you are on the platform, the more likely businesses will find you. After that, it's up to you to broker a deal. I can't promise you five-figure speaking gigs or that you'll land a traditional publishing deal. I can assure you since Microsoft owns LinkedIn, they're here to stay. Set up your profile and get started today!

*A*ccording to various online sources, over 80% of online traffic in 2021 will be video.[11] People are consuming video in mass quantities. If you aren't part of the movement, you'll be at a greater disadvantage than those who are.

I'd more recently seen an old-school self-publisher tout how he felt it was a waste of time and resources. That's easy for him to say since he's spent years building his author platform, and he had the advantage of a simpler algorithm to contend with when he began. Now, it's a different game. He's the exception to the rule and has the advantage of opting out of video. The rest of us need to scrap for the readers we want and need to retain. Video is one of the easiest and most cost-effective solutions to promoting your books and author brand.

Where you have to spend thousands of dollars simply to learn how to advertise, video doesn't require much more than whatever resources you currently have. All you need is:

- A stable internet connection

- A camera — a webcam or your mobile phone camera will do

- A microphone — again, anything readily available will do. In most instances, an onboard microphone in your PC or phone is sufficient.

- Good lighting — don't take this lightly. You can make a horrible camera look like a million bucks with the right amount of lighting. Shoot with ambient daylight if you don't have adequate lighting. If not, you can always use table lamps.

- Willingness to learn the process of creating better video

Don't worry about creating cinematic masterpieces. The whole issue people get hung up on is creating perfection. The further you can make it from perfect at first, the better. As your author presence grows and you get more funding, you can upgrade your videos. Until then, stick with what you have.

Also, don't worry about the type of video editing software. If you do use editing software, simply search up free options based on your operating system. If you're using iOS, then search up "free video editing software" on your iPhone. If you're using PC, search for "free video editing software for Windows." There are so many free options it'd be crazy for you to plunk down hundreds on software that'll merely slow down your process of marketing and promoting your book.

Outside of the previous recommendations around social media (i.e., Facebook, Twitter, Instagram, LinkedIn, etc.), consider the king of all video platforms to be YouTube and its live-streaming competitor, Twitch. Both platforms are at the forefront of online video. And, if you want to reach the most viewers you can so you can win them over as readers, then you have to leverage these avenues.

YouTube and Twitch have their share of pros and cons. While it's not my place to tell you to use one platform over the other, I want to showcase why you should consider either avenue. There's no better time than now to begin creating videos on YouTube or Twitch.

The Art of YouTube for Authors

YouTube has the benefit and direct relationship with the world's most utilized search engine in Google.[12] If you can become discoverable through Google, then you've got it made. While it's not impossible to build and grow a platform on YouTube, it will be hard at first. Once you get the hang of shooting and uploading videos on YouTube, the rest becomes more manageable.

The name of the game on YouTube is – watch time. The longer you can get viewers to consume your content on YouTube, the more discoverable your videos become. This comes with a bit of a catch, though. You need to get people to watch your video, and the barrier of entry can seem impossible. If you want YouTube to serve your video to viewers, you need to have a good thumbnail and enticing title. Once a viewer clicks on your thumbnail to view your content, the next hurdle to overcome is watch time. After they start watching your content for prolonged periods, you're in like Flynn.

A few things to take into consideration when uploading a video:

1. **Keyword selection** — use relevant keywords in your title, description, and tags.

2. **Links** — though YouTube doesn't like you sending viewers off the platform, it's still a good idea to promote your books and author website. Don't go overboard on the outbound links.

3. **Pinned comment** — engagement is key, like any other social media platform, so lead with a relevant and thought-provoking question. Then, send your viewers to a previous video of yours. It creates an endless loop once you have a backlog of videos. If

1. you're new to YouTube and don't have many videos, include links to your latest book or website.

2. **Encourage engagement** — in the video, encourage viewers to leave comments by asking a pertinent question. Much like what we did on Facebook, you'll want to do the same on YouTube. Get in the last word by answering every comment. This sends small signals to the YouTube algorithm and bolsters the relevance of your video.

3. **Miscellaneous engagement** – Also, consider mentioning other ways to engage, including liking, disliking, sharing, or subscribing. Just don't overload viewers with too many requests. I usually stick to one per video, and I'll load it up at the beginning or the end.

When it comes to publishing videos on YouTube, be patient! Rome wasn't built overnight, and you're going to need the flexibility to succeed on this platform. Since you're using YouTube to grow your author brand, remember to always lead with it. This simple framework has served me well:

1. Lead with the topic of the video.

2. Introduce yourself and tell people who you are and what you do. Brevity is critical here. So, you can say something like:

   A. Hey, I'm Dale L. Roberts, a bestselling author and self-publishing advocate who wants to show you how to publish books that sell.

3. Go right into your content. Don't delay. YouTube viewers tend to be a bit more impatient and want their goods without all the jib-jab.

1. As you wrap up your content, direct people to another of your videos. At first, you won't have many, if any, videos to send them. Direct them to a link in your description or your pinned comment. When I wrap up a video, I avoid closing words like "in conclusion" or "that's it." Because most viewers will leave your video right then and there. Whatever you say after those closing words will be wasted breath.

Are Book Trailers Effective?

Can a book trailer be a useful promotional piece on YouTube? Are book trailers a good way to drive more sales and build awareness of your author brand? The answer will shock you.

Yes and no.

In most instances, the old-fashioned way of promoting your publication through book trailers is antiquated. Back when online video was big, and ebooks were at the forefront of self-publishing, sure, book trailers were effective. Now, video publishing is more popular. It's going to take much more than some flashy trailer you bought from a seller on Fiverr. Will that book trailer ever work? It's certainly debatable. You could use it in paid promotions through YouTube ads or even in Facebook Ads, but you'll need to know how to use those platforms first. Also, you'll have to fork up a pretty penny just to get it in front of your target audience.

Even then, there are no guarantees. In most instances, the traditional book trailer is dead. It's tired, played out, and most people will tune it out or turn to other channels with cat videos or blooper reels. You only get one chance to make the first impression on your viewers.

To make an impact, state how you are the go-to author and wrote the premier book in your niche. How do you do that? Think outside the box. Mat Best, the author of *Thank You for My Service*, did just that. Instead of making the physical book the talking point, Best spun a humorous narrative through video. Between loud guns, scantily clad women, and over-the-top shenanigans, he nailed it when it came to stopping the scroll.

Mat Best created a highly memorable book
trailer that went viral on YouTube.

I'm not telling you to do the same thing. It won't make any sense if you're a children's book author producing a video like Mat Best. What you'll need to do is think like this:

> How can I showcase the content of my book
> in a way that commands attention?
>
> What will leave a lasting impression on casual viewers?
>
> What are a few things my ideal audience can relate
> to within a good thirty to sixty-second video?

Now, to his credit, Mat Best probably has deeper pockets than most indie authors. You might have to be resourceful. If you need any further inspiration on how little you need to create videos that take off, watch any video by comedian Gus Johnson or Caleb City. These two creators use nothing more than their camera, point, and then shoot. That's it!

As a creative entrepreneur, if you're going to create and publish a book trailer, make it worth everyone's time. Remember, if you take your time brainstorming concepts, you'll find it will be evergreen content. The longer the video is on the platform, the more views it'll get in due time. The more views and watch time a video gets, the more viewers will see it over the long haul.

If you find recording video to be overwhelming, then you may want to consider live streaming video on Twitch.

The Game of Live Video on Twitch

According to Wired.com, Twitch had over 1.5 billion watch time hours of live video in April 2020.[13] Compare this to YouTube, who merely had 461 million watch time hours of live video. Twitch is fast becoming the go-to source for live streaming video. Even though Twitch began as a live streaming platform for gamers, it quickly evolved after Amazon acquired it for nearly $1 billion.[14] Even the world's largest and most successful online retailer saw something on this platform. Still, they knew they were getting into a market that needed some more guidance to appeal to a broader audience.

Fast forward to today, and you'll find the most successful live streaming content creators are outside of the gaming realm. Scores of authors, including me, are now streaming their content on Twitch. They're doing everything from IRL (in real life) to writing sprints to book reviews and beyond. Twitch embraces and even showcases the creative entrepreneur.

There's one catch when it comes to streaming on Twitch. BYOA – bring your own audience. Despite the platform owners, Amazon, having one of the most sophisticated search engines on the market, Twitch doesn't have much of a search engine. It bases relevance on how many concurrent viewers are consuming and engaging in your content, which is just a popularity contest. As an example, you're streaming a book reading on your channel and have three viewers. At the same time, another author is streaming a book reading and has forty viewers. The Twitch search engine will serve the latter channel over your channel based on the sheer volume of active viewers.

Not to be confused, Twitch won't take away from your viewers. Still, they're less apt to add any more people to your stream based on your performance compared to other channels streaming similar content.

It would behoove you to gather as many friends, family, and fans to join you for your streams. Build as much awareness as possible for each live stream. Do not take this lightly. You must bring your own audience or face the sad music of streaming to no one. Promote your live streams on social media and send out details to your email list.

What exactly can you do to market and promote your books on Twitch? Simply being visible isn't enough to get people to buy your books. I'd recommend considering a few of these ideas to grease your creative wheels and get your live stream going:

- **Write-alongs** — this largely depends on how comfortable you are in sharing your content. You can screen share your manuscript as you type it out. If you're worried about pirates stealing your content,

- relax. You're essentially creating a copyright by video, and this can be admissible evidence should you need to escalate litigation.

  > Fans watching get to have a sneak peek into your upcoming work. The more of a backlog you build, the more invested they'll be in your live streams.

  > You get bonus points if you involve your community in the direction of your manuscript. Write-alongs are a great way to break writer's block since you have a little outside influence in the creative process.

- **Live writing sprints** — other writers might want to join you while you write. It's one of the best ways to keep you focused while working on a time crunch. I'm doing it right now with this book.

  > You can do live writing sprints two ways — with or without a screen share of the manuscript. Either way, you can always cue up a stopwatch or timer. Once the time passes, let your viewers know.

- **Advanced readings** — read your latest manuscript or segments of a book.

- **Gaming sessions** — have your followers join you for fun games. As a reward, you can gift out copies of your latest book — ebook, print book, or audiobook. It's entirely up to you. People love games and getting rewards for participating.

- **AMA** — ask me anything is a fun way for followers to get a sense of who you are.

What you stream on Twitch is only limited to your imagination. Just remember, if you want to get any real traction on this platform, you must be consistent and invite people to the party.

If you have a Twitch profile set up, interweave your books and writing through the channel graphics, including the channel art, panels, and outbound links. A great way to advertise while you stream without having the hassle of typing out the comments is with a stream bot. You can look up any number of free services that'll integrate with your live stream. I currently use StreamElements to manage my stream bot. All I had to do was add a few lines of copy, set when to release the comment, and include special considerations for posting a comment. It's way easier than you know and can be effective in passive marketing.

Most of your viewers won't even realize it's a bot. Since it's promoting your work, naturally, your viewers will be more inclined to check it out. Just remember, a little goes a long way. You don't want your bot beating up viewers in the chat every five minutes with your latest werebear shapeshifter romance novel. Have your bot post about once per hour. Put yourself in your viewers' shoes, and you'll know how much is enough.

Other Live Streaming Alternatives

Could you live stream anywhere else besides Twitch? Absolutely! It's entirely up to you on where you want to stream. Some great places to start:

- YouTube

- Facebook Live

- Periscope

- Instagram Live

- LinkedIn Live

The key to gaining any traction in live video is staying consistent. Viewers appreciate a regular schedule and full transparency. You can't expect to get great results if you stream at sporadic and unpredictable times. If you have no choice than to stream whenever life allows you then, I'd recommend promoting an email notification squad. Announce to your live audience you'll send them notifications and a schedule of live broadcasts. That way, they can join and support you for any upcoming broadcasts.

Of course, having an email notification squad is great for regular streamers too. Still, it's not as essential as it is for streamers who are not consistent. The email list can be your saving grace and a great way to get feedback from your current viewing audience.

Are you stuck on what times or days you should live stream? Then, ask your email list. It's tough to get a clear answer from your audience if you're live streaming. After all, if they're watching you, then chances are pretty likely that's a good day and time. You want to get a more overhead view of what everyone prefers.

Once you have a good idea of the best times to stream, adjust your schedule accordingly. Then, you avoid streaming to no one every time you go live. It can feel defeating enough as it is when streaming to no one. To make matters worse is when you have an audience, but no one comes to see you live.

Save yourself the heartache and start an email list for your notification squad. Then, when you go live, you can gather as a community and have a great time!

Promotion ▾	Amazon Advertising

*H*ere's the part everyone inevitably skips to because it seems like the most straightforward steps in marketing and promoting a book. I implore you to visit the previous options before ever considering this avenue. Why? Because the earlier options can be free and cost way less. There's far more risk when putting your hard-earned money into paid advertising.

Clearly, this chapter will not be an exhaustive overview of Amazon Advertising. I'm going to give you enough information to be dangerous. Consider reviewing the resources in the back of the book for deeper dives into Amazon Advertising. Certainly, I don't want you to skip this chapter, because if you're new to Amazon Ads, then this is the best first steps to using the platform.

Why Amazon Advertising?

Amazon is a gigantic marketplace with billions of products. With every passing day, millions more products flood the market. It's no surprise how authors publish books only to see their titles drop into obscurity. Gone are the days when you could simply publish and pray for the best. This retail platform is hyper-competitive. Amazon Advertising is one of the best ways to be seen and heard above the noise.

Many experts will argue how Facebook Ads or Google Ads are more effective than Amazon Ads. Though Amazon Advertising is somewhat archaic compared to its predecessors, Facebook, and Google, it's come a long way over the past two years. I'd even gamble to say by the time you're reading this, the features and availability have improved immensely. Why? Amazon loves money. They don't just love the customer's money; they love your money too.

Amazon Advertising is simply another vehicle for the retailer to gather customers. Make no mistake about it, Amazon wants you to succeed. If you make money through advertising your books on their platform, then they make money. However, they're not losing anything if you dump money blindly into advertising campaigns yielding no results. They're not going to give you a polite email telling you what you're doing wrong. The amount of resources on creating better ad campaigns is embarrassingly low for Amazon.

That's why it's on you to learn this platform as you go. Quite a few would-be experts will have you believe there's a magic formula of used keywords, cost-per-click, and ad launch day that works best. All of them are wrong, but some of their information bears merit in your advertising campaigns.

For now, the best first step for any newbie is to consider what you can afford to lose. Yes, I didn't mistype that. When starting any type of advertising, you need to go in with the expectation to lose money. After all, if you've never used Amazon Advertising before, it's going to take time for you to get used to the platform. If you have experience in Google Ads or Facebook Ads, you're at a greater advantage.

Nonetheless, invest money you can stand to lose. I'll explain a more practical strategy and give you an action plan based on what works best for your budget. Rest assured, I will not recommend you spend hundreds of dollars per day. You'll be shocked at how low I recommend you set your budget. Before we dive into what to spend, it's important to know the most essential metrics.

Impressions, Clicks & Sales, Oh My!

When running an ad campaign on a book, there are three powerful metrics you have to pay the closest attention to, including:

1. Impressions — when Amazon serves your ad to a customer. If Amazon places your ad in front of a customer, then that counts as an impression. The best part about impressions — they're free.

2. Clicks — are when the browsing customer clicks on your ad to see more about your book. Clicks determine the success of your ad.

3. Sales — are the ultimate metric. When you can nail this metric, you've mastered Amazon Ads.

However, none of these metrics mean squat if you don't have a grasp on what to spend. It'd be nice if we could simply pay x-amount of dollars per month and get our ads served. It doesn't work that way. You have to go into Amazon Ads with a competitive mindset. You are vying for customers' attention, while millions of other authors are doing the same.

Determining the Cost Per Click

When you set up an ad, Amazon Advertising will ask how much you are willing to pay per click. Being a newbie, it can be overwhelming. What does a click cost? How much is a decent price to get a customer's attention? Why do you have to even guess in the first place?

First, you should never, under any circumstances, use the suggested bid feature. It's essentially like letting Amazon reach into your pocket and take what they want. In most cases, these bids are absurdly high. The return on investment will be marginal at best, and in some instances, a complete loss.

Amazon Advertising acts as a real-time auction-based system. Imagine millions of authors bidding for millions of ad placement types. Unlike any real-world auction, Amazon plays by a different set of rules. Though an auction typically favors the highest bidder, Amazon Advertising is a bit trickier. Since an algorithm runs Amazon search, the ads platform leans heavily on it for determining the most favorable outcome for the customer.

In my book, *Amazon Keyword for Books*, I discussed the complexity of the Amazon algorithm. To summarize it, Amazon favors books it deems relevant. They base algorithmic relevance on sales, product page engagement, and several other factors. The primary driving force in determining algorithmic relevance is sales. If a book sells, Amazon deems it more relevant than a book that does not drive sales. These are the cold, hard facts here, folks.

That is largely why Amazon Ads give a slight advantage to authors who use it than those who don't. Ads, in theory, build awareness and hopefully drive sales. More sales equate to more relevancy in the Amazon algorithm.

In the real-time, auction-based system, you're vying for the coveted placement in front of the customer through a specific keyword, product placement, or delivery type. You're not the only one. Others want that same spot at the very same time. Rather than give everyone a participation trophy, Amazon has to play favorites. Ad placement is an algorithmic-driven decision.

As a rough example, John and Pam publish books in the yogurt niche. John's book sells about twelve copies per day, and Pam's book sells only one copy per day. For the keyword "yogurt," John bids thirty-five cents, and Pam bids ninety-five cents. In a real-world auction, Pam would win since she bid the highest. On Amazon, the winning bid goes to the product with more relevance. Since John has a proven seller in the niche, Amazon will lean in favor of his book versus Pam's book. Pam doesn't go home empty-handed, though. Her book might still bear relevance so that she might get second servings after John. That means John's ad will get better placement, while Pam's ad will get placement after John.

Here's the cool thing. Because John won the auction, no one has to pay above that amount. Rather than spending ninety-five cents for her placement, Pam will pay under the amount John bid. Pretty cool, right? However, I've minimized a rather complex topic that does have more variables in it.

When it comes to determining your cost-per-click, see what Amazon suggests. You need to figure out what cost makes the most sense from an odds standpoint. I base a large motivating factor on how I dial in my cost-per-click on the net profit of a given book.

Here's a rough example that paints a basic picture: my book is $19.95, and the net profit is $6.97. Now I'm going to figure out what I'm willing to lose from the net profit to get a decent return on my investment. In theory, I profit $6.97 per sale of a book, so I should be able to spend up to $6.97 before I become concerned. The issue lies in how I bid. If I place a bid at $1 cost-per-click (CPC), I will only get seven clicks to get a sale and remain at the break-even point.

However, if I bid seventy cents per click, I can get up to ten clicks. I have three more opportunities to turn a profit. What if I bid only seven cents per click? Then, I could get up to one-hundred clicks to turn a profit. The issue is on the real-time auction. Bidding too low won't even get your ad served anywhere. It's almost like showing up to a formal dinner party in jean shorts and a cutoff. You won't be well-received, and most people are going to avoid you like the plague. Amazon won't serve your ad anywhere since the more relevant books are taking higher placement based on a higher bid.

There are only so many spots Amazon can offer to advertisers before they are all filled up. If you aren't speaking the same language as others are in your niche, you won't get a single impression. If you find you aren't getting many impressions, then adjust your bid upward. Only move it up slightly, and don't go overboard. Let's say you have a keyword bid at 7¢, and you aren't getting impressions. Move it up to 10¢ to 12¢ to see if that will open things up.

When starting in ads, it will take time to get a sense of what to expect and bid in your chosen niche. Don't expect to win them all. Some ads will be winners, while others are going to be duds.

If your impressions are up, then you're bidding at an optimal level. Let's say you're getting tons of impressions but no clicks. What do you do then? You have to analyze two areas:

1. **Book cover** — is your book cover as great as you think it is? Measure it up against other books in your niche. If it matches the niche, then you're good. If it sticks out like a sore thumb, then you need to change it.

2. **Relevance** — Is the keyword or product you selected relevant to your book? Even though you might think "military science fiction" is an excellent keyword for your book, that doesn't mean customers agree with you.

However, if you find you're getting clicks with no sales, then you have one of two problems:

1. **Book description** — the most significant barrier of entry in customers visiting your product page is your cover. Once they get there, you need to entice them to buy or stand to lose them. If you're getting the visitors, but not getting the sales, you've got a book description problem.

2. **Customer disconnect** — Sometimes, customers will unwittingly click an ad. In some cases, they're simply window shopping, and you get to foot the bill for their tire-kicking ways. Analyze the keyword or product choice in your ad to determine if you should keep spending money serving that audience.

Once you've gotten the impressions, the clicks, and the buys going, you shouldn't have any issues. As long as you've kept your bid at a reasonable level, you should see a return. If you don't see a return, then nix what's blowing through your daily budget. That leads me to the most crucial part of advertising – your daily budget.

Determining Your Daily Budget

This is the single most misunderstood part of advertising on Amazon. Most authors assume if they have the money, then customers will come. Unless you know what you're doing, you're essentially handing over your money to Amazon, and they won't question it.

I cannot overstate this enough, so let's repeat it for emphasis. Do not invest more than you are willing to lose in advertising. If you're new to Amazon Ads, you need to invest the money as if you're paying for an education. Don't spend it blindly or expect to learn through osmosis. You're going to need to monitor your ads daily, analyze the performance, adjust the bids, pause low-performing keywords or products, and check your search terms report. Every day you should be picking up small hints on what's working for your ad and what isn't working.

As a baseline, I'd recommend starting at a daily budget at $1 to $10 per day. I know Amazon recommends you start with $10 per day, but they don't forbid you from running at $1, so start low. Here's your new motto when it comes to advertising anywhere:

> Start low, scale slow.

Instead of throwing countless dollars down the drain and hoping for the best, you're going to invest your money wisely. It all starts with keeping your daily ad spend as low as you can handle for the next thirty to ninety days. If you do not have enough money to invest in ads for the next month, don't start. If you do the math behind it, at a daily ad spend of $1 per day over thirty to ninety days, you'll spend $30 to $90. On the higher end of things, at a daily ad spend of $10 per day over the same period, you'll pay $300 to $900.

For your first ads, keep your bids extremely low. You're going to make even those extreme coupon clippers and spendthrifts blush at how low you bid. While some people flex on how much money they blow on ads, you'll brag about how little you spend. I generally start with about 10¢ to 15¢ cost-per-click (CPC). Again, forget about the suggested bid and just start with a low CPC.

If you aren't seeing any impressions in the first seven days, you'll need to increase your CPC. Move up the CPC by about 2¢ to 5¢. Give it another week before you move it higher. Only move up bids on non-performing keywords. If a keyword is getting hundreds to thousands of impressions in the first week, you're on the right track.

If you see impressions and clicks, but no sales, then analyze the data first. If it's a simple case of only a few clicks and no buys, you don't have enough data to prove any statistical relevance. As an example:

- Neutral Results
  - Keyword: bow staffs for children = 1,000 impressions, 10 clicks, 0 sales
    - This is just not enough data to determine its effectiveness
- Bad Results
  - Keyword: bow staffs for kids = 1,000 impressions, 100 clicks, 0 sales
    - This keyword is a dud. If you aren't converting at least one out of a hundred clicks, then you've got a problem with the keyword selection or the book description.
- Good Results
  - Keyword: bow staffs for toddlers = 1,000 impressions, 100 clicks, 10 sales
    - This keyword is good as long as your CPC isn't too high. You're converting one out of every ten clicks, or about 10% of all customers. If you can convert at an even better rate, then you're off to the races!

It will take time for you to get an idea of what keywords perform good and bad. Then, you can pause all bad keywords and then toss them into your negative keywords as an exact match. That way, any customer searching with that given keyword will not see your ad. After all, if the keyword performs poorly, you don't want to keep paying for it.

The Research Ad

Every ad you start should begin with a research ad: a campaign that simply tests the waters. You'll want to activate a sponsored product ad and use manual keywords. You're allowed to have up to 1,000 keywords, but don't use all 1,000 slots. I used to lean heavily in filling all of the keyword slots; however, it leaves little wiggle room for you to add to a campaign that may take off. Stick with 500 to 800 keywords.

All ad campaigns have a certain amount of shelf life before they run out of steam. I've had some ads perform well for up to a year at a time while others ran well for ninety days and petered out. Sadly, I can't explain this anomaly, but you safeguard your campaign once you leave a little wiggle room.

As an ad starts, you'll see the impressions, clicks, and sales come through. Pay the closest attention to the clicks and sales. Once you see a click or sale, go to your **Search Terms** report. Find out what the customer searched for when they found your ad. If you were using a broad keyword, you'd likely see some variation of that associated with your ad.

Customer search term	Keywords	Match type	Clicks	Spend	CPC
Total 39			49	$11.73	$0.24
manon mathews	manon mathews	Exact	1	$0.09	$0.09
calisthenics dvd training	calisthenics	Phrase	1	$0.24	$0.24
foam rolling	foam rolling	Exact	1	$0.21	$0.21
women workout books	workout	Phrase	1	$0.23	$0.23
100 workouts without equipment	workouts without equipment	Phrase	1	$0.45	$0.45
aaron alexander align book	aaron alexander	Phrase	1	$0.44	$0.44
bigger leaner stronger	bigger leaner stronger	Exact	1	$0.25	$0.25
blandine calais germain	blandine calais germain	Exact	1	$0.20	$0.20
book core exercises	core exercises	Phrase	1	$0.45	$0.45
calisthenics workout book	workout	Phrase	1	$0.10	$0.10
calisthenics	calisthenics	Exact	3	$0.62	$0.21

The Search Terms report shows what customers search when they discover your book.

Using the same theory we did for determining the rough statistical relevance, we'll do the same with your search term report. Is the keyword converting into a sale? If so, copy the keyword, make a note of the CPC, add it to your campaign as an exact match, and if you're feeling bold, the phrase match. This is your way of declaring to Amazon, "I only want people who say (insert your exact keyword here) to see my ad."

With the phrase match, you're telling Amazon, "I only want people to see my ad who say (insert your phrase keyword here) with a little bit of deviation."

As a rough example, if your phrase match keyword is "paranormal romance," then the ad might be seen by customers who search:

- **Paranormal romance** for teens

- Shapeshifter **paranormal romance**

- Werebear **paranormal romance** for teens

Keep in mind that these are just rough examples, not an exhaustive list of all the variations related to the exact phrase match of "paranormal romance." As you can imagine, the combinations of "paranormal romance" and other words are limitless.

Now, it's natural for you to wonder - where do you get the keywords? There's a variety of ways you can do it. In my first book in this series, *Amazon Keywords for Books*, I discussed finding all the right keywords. The best way to build a list of 500 to 800 keywords is with a keyword research tool. Spending countless hours coming up with that many keywords is insane. If you want a no-cost tool, then look into Google Ads' Keyword Planner. You'll have to jump through a few hoops to secure a Google Ads account, but once you do, you should be able to use their keyword planner 100% free of charge.

Google and the Google logo are registered trademarks of Google LLC, used with permission.

The Google Ads Keyword Planner is an excellent resource for finding plenty of keywords fast.

Simply enter a keyword into the Keyword Planner, and you'll get scores of related keywords. Download the spreadsheet. Then, copy and paste all the keywords into an Amazon Ads campaign. Before adding all the keywords, be sure to switch the setting to "Custom Bid" and set your bid low. Again, we're just doing a research ad.

Why do I start all ad campaigns for my books with a research ad? I can uncover the low hanging fruit while building relevance for my books and ads. Quite a few keywords are untapped, and no one is bidding on them. While everyone else is fighting for scraps on the competitive keywords, you can be unearthing the diamonds in the rough.

For example, when I used Publisher Rocket (see more in the resources section) for my book, *The 90-Day Home Workout Plan*, I kept getting the keyword "penis enlargement." Naturally, my book has nothing to do with male genitalia. For whatever reason, Publisher Rocket felt I needed to add "penis enlargement" to my ad campaigns. Fair enough, I thought. I finally gave in and let it go through. I started at an absurdly low bid of 8¢.

Out of the gate, I didn't get many impressions at all. I didn't see much action at all with that keyword, but once I got a click, I got a sale. That went on for months. Without fail, every time I got a click, I got a sale. We can speculate on why a customer would want my book based on that keyword, but the bottom line is it worked. What is the best part? It converted at 8¢ CPC. The net profit for every book, including the ad spend, was $6.89. Yes, "penis enlargement" wasn't what I imagined as being relevant to my book. Once I found the unusual keyword converted, I wasn't going to argue.

Now, I'm not telling you to find racy or edgy words to add to your campaigns. This story is more to illustrate a point. While most people fought for ad placement with "exercise" or "workouts" from 25¢ to $1.50, I selected more obscure keywords. My competitors spent more and profited less while I profited more while risking less. That's the ticket with research ads. You want to find the keywords no one else is using and bid low enough to get placement and convert to sales.

Once you get enough of these small victories, it adds up. Your title becomes more relevant, and when you go to battle other authors in your space for ad placement, you're more apt to win the bid without having to break the bank.

When it comes to Amazon Advertising, there are a few rules you must honor:

1. Never invest what you can't stand to lose.

2. Monitor all ads daily.

3. Adjust every campaign to mitigate any unnecessary spending.

4. When one ad dies, put another in its place.

To be clear, Amazon Advertising is not for everyone. If you aren't patient enough to learn how to use this tool, then don't. If you can't dedicate at least fifteen to thirty minutes a day to learning the system and tweaking your ads, then don't do it. However, if you have the discretionary expense, the time, and the willingness, Amazon Advertising might be for you. Again, for a more in-depth look into advertising on Amazon, visit the resources in the back of this book.

*T*he more visible you make yourself, the more opportunities people get to know who you are and what you do. Author appearances should be integral to every author's marketing plan. If you do not currently have author appearances as part of your plan, it's time to change that.

I understand some authors don't like to be in the public eye. Some break out in hives at the thought of being seen. It's much easier than you know if you only get out of your own way and get in front of more people. Where do you start, and what do you need?

What You'll Need First — The Press Kit

*F*or many new authors, you're going to have a tough time whipping this part together. With a little creativity and an ability to humblebrag, you can do it. Before you reach out to anyone about doing anything or appearing in any capacity, you'll need a press kit.

Your press kit should include these four things. I'll elaborate below:

1. One or two headshots

2. A short bio

3. Relevant links

4. BONUS: Media roll

The headshot needs to be professional and should not be a selfie. If you can't afford a professional photographer, then have a friend take a picture of you in a well-lit area with minimal background distractions. Do not skimp on the resolution or quality. This means your old-school flip phone won't cut it. However, if you have an iPhone 11 or any recent smartphone, you have a good camera for shooting a picture.

You should be the focal point of the shot and not the pile of dirty clothes in the background. Remember, you want people to perceive you as a professional. A little smile goes a long way, so lighten up a little bit. That is, unless you're writing dark horror suspense novels. In that case, appear brooding and troubled.

Once you have a good shot, you'll need it in two different formats. Keep one file in the original quality. Convert the next one to a PNG with a transparent background. If you're familiar with graphic design software, then this should be an easy fix. If you don't know how to do it yourself, you can outsource this task or find an online tool. Again, resources are in the back, including the services I prefer.

When it comes to your biography, keep it short and sweet. One or two hundred words will suffice. Any more is too much for your prospects to read and digest. You want short, punchy ad copy that leaves a lasting impression. Make sure you aren't covering the story of your life. Speak only about things relevant to your niche.

In my bio, I don't bother sharing what college I went to, how I grew up in a military family, or that I'm a former professional wrestler. Though my backstory is interesting in an interview, it's not the best first impression I want to make.

Next, you need to tell people where to find you. Don't go overboard. Less is more. Lead with your most important website to your least important. In some instances, having too many links will overwhelm a host. Naturally, they might select the first one and call it done. I'd recommend leading with your author website. Follow it up with any social media links. It is entirely up to you where you wish to drive traffic. Only send people to sites where you are currently active. Don't send someone to LinkedIn if you never use it. Send them to places you are active and have more examples of how awesome you are.

Save your author bio and relevant links on one document. You can do it on a standard document file or to a PDF. Dress it up on Canva or by ordering a service through Fiverr. I like to save my bio and links sheet as a document (i.e., .doc or .docx). When I need to edit, I can do those quickly without having to redo some fancy PDF. I don't sweat this area too much because the next option is where I throw in the wow factor.

The media roll is a fancy breakdown of all the things a prospect can expect from you. Remember how I told you to go easy on your bio. That's because now we're going to lay it on thick.

The media roll is a compilation of the press kit. Now you're going to include a few other pertinent talking points. Include your headshot and other pictures of you in the wild. That way, they know you aren't just some stuffy writer. Next, include your bio, any accolades or awards you earned, and your experience level. Do not take your experience level lightly. You don't need to fluff it up or dress it down. Sometimes, people are looking for a specific level of experience, so you don't want to put yourself into situations you cannot handle.

Though it's a bit daunting at first for newbies, include your social media reach. Showcase the platforms you're actively using and the followers you amassed. Include your handles and your links so people can easily access your social media platforms. Do not worry about how many followers you have. In some instances, people are more interested in how active you are and what type of engagement you get.

In an interview on the Restream YouTube channel (DaleLinks.com/RestreamInterview), the Head of Partnerships at Restream addressed a viewer question about what companies consider when finding a good fit. Her big insight was she didn't care about how many followers someone has. She only focused on community engagement. That's powerful! If you're hosting a party of a hundred people, and no one is dancing, then some prospects might pass working with you.

It's better to have a party of ten where everyone is going buck wild and having a good time. This means you're a great party host, and more people are bound to join you in due time.

Speaking of being quite the host, gather any testimonials, reviews, or positive words about you. Of course, don't fake it. If you've had an excellent review of your book or a client who raves about you, then the media roll is a place to showcase it. Three to four testimonials are sufficient, with about two to three short sentences about you.

The last step is critical to making a good first impression. You must convert your media roll into a short yet eye-catching report. For the bio and relevant links, it's okay to have a simple document, but for the media roll, you need to pull out all stops. I used Canva to create mine and did it within thirty minutes. Now and then, I update the media roll with the latest stats, which only takes me about five minutes. If you have neither the time nor patience to do it yourself, hire out. Every person I hand off my media roll to remarks on how much they liked it. You'll thank me later when you put a little time into this asset.

SELF PUBLISHING WITH DALE

indie author

ABOUT ME

After plying my trade as a writer in the world of indie publishing, I decided to pay it forward and share my insights with other authors in the publishing community.

Since starting Self-Publishing with Dale on YouTube in 2016, my educational videos amassed over 1.5 million views and helped countless authors and self-publishers build a rock-solid publishing business.

39.2K
YOUTUBE SUBSCRIBERS
Since April 2016

2K
TWITTER FOLLOWERS
Since May 2017

4K
FACEBOOK GROUP MEMBERS
Since June 2018

About my brand

SELF-PUBLISHING WITH DALE

I share new content weekly on YouTube and host one live stream for self-publishers every Monday at 12pm EDT on Twitch.

In the process of growing a community on YouTube and Twitch, I've built and grown an active following of over 4,000 members in the Facebook Groups called Self-Publishing Books and the DIY Publishing Course Community.

187

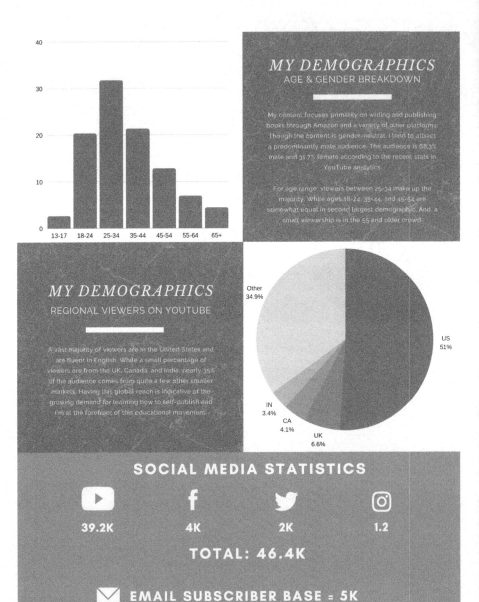

MY DEMOGRAPHICS
AGE & GENDER BREAKDOWN

My content focuses primarily on writing and publishing books through Amazon and a variety of other platforms. Though the content is gender-neutral, I tend to attract a predominantly male audience. The audience is 68.3% male and 31.7% female according to the recent stats in YouTube analytics.

For age range, viewers between 25-34 make up the majority. While ages 18-24, 35-44, and 45-54 are somewhat equal in second largest demographic. And a small viewership is in the 55 and older crowd.

MY DEMOGRAPHICS
REGIONAL VIEWERS ON YOUTUBE

A vast majority of viewers are in the United States and are fluent in English. While a small percentage of viewers are from the UK, Canada, and India, nearly 35% of the audience comes from quite a few other smaller markets. Having this global reach is indicative of the growing demand for learning how to self-publish and I'm at the forefront of this educational movement.

Other 34.9%
US 51%
IN 3.4%
CA 4.1%
UK 6.6%

SOCIAL MEDIA STATISTICS

39.2K   4K   2K   1.2

TOTAL: 46.4K

EMAIL SUBSCRIBER BASE = 5K

DALE L.
ROBERTS

SELF-PUBLISHING EXPERT &
VIDEO CONTENT CREATOR

CONTACT DALE

614-555-5555
dale@selfpublishingwithdale.com
www.selfpublishingwithdale.com

youtube.com/selfpublishingwithdale

twitter.com/selfpubwithdale

facebook.com/selfpubwithdale

instagram.com/selfpubwithdale

YOUTUBE STATS AT A GLANCE

MONTHLY AVERAGE
Views: 93.1k
Watch time minutes: 497.8k
Audience growth: 1.5k

TOTAL
Views: 2.1m
Watch time minutes: 10.8m
Subscribers: 39.2k

SEE WHAT OTHERS SAY ABOUT DALE...

"The best thing to happen to my self-publishing business was stumbling onto Dale's YouTube channel."
-Moninque "Mojo" Siedlak, indie author

"His straight to the point approach is appreciated and has an in-depth knowledge of the industry few offer."
-Darrin Wiggins, indie publisher

"Although I've been publishing books in Amazon since 2011, I found Dale's YouTube channel over a year ago and immediately recognized his great talent: not only as an expert self-publisher but also as teacher and communicator."
-Alvaro Parra Pinto, YouTube Video Creator & Indie Author

"Dale has been called a guru, a label that I know he dislikes, but in my self-publishing business he is simply my mentor and friend."
-Mark Brownless, Indie Author

"Dale L. Roberts is an amazing, generous and helpful person who has a true knowledge of the publishing business."
-Anna Nadler, Indie Publisher

You will not have to invest a ton of money. In fact, I wouldn't recommend investing much, if any, money at all. I'm a spendthrift at heart and recommend using free resources like Canva or GIMP to get the job done. When push comes to shove, and you're short on time or energy, outsource!

The last vital step in the press kit assembly is uploading to a cloud drive. You'll want to store all your items in one folder with a shareable link. With that shareable link, create a short link. Bitly has a free service for link shortening. Even better, WordPress has a free plugin called Pretty Links. It essentially creates a subdirectory on your own domain that redirects to the shareable link you created. If you don't have WordPress, but own a domain name, visit your domain name service provider, and ask them to set you up with a subdomain that redirects to your given link. Most services provide unlimited subdomains at no extra cost.

Examples:

1. Bitly Link — bit.ly/bookreview

2. Subdirectory — dalelinks.com/marketingbook

3. Subdomain — marketingbook.dalelinks.com

Whatever you do, avoid sending the full, unedited link. It reeks of amateur hour, and it's also not something a prospect will easily remember later. It's easier to remember your author-specific website or bitly link.

Media Appearances

Under the media appearances umbrella, we're going to focus on various ways you can reach your audience. It's not solely limited to being on television or getting a YouTube channel for an interview. We'll find a host of options that will benefit your author brand.

To clarify, media appearances on their own will not sell a ton of books. The process of landing media appearances can seem overwhelming, and your ego may take a hit when you see your book sales don't move much. That's okay because we're focusing on the long-term goal. Appearing in front of as many people as possible builds awareness of who you are and what you do. It takes up to eight interactions with any one person before you develop a sense of trust.[15]

Chances are likely if you're appearing on the local morning show, viewers are seeing you for the first time. Naturally, you'll think the interview went well, and your interviewers might even remark on how well you did. The reality is it's going to take much more than a single appearance on a morning show before anyone will rush to buy your book. Sure, there are exceptions to the rule. For the vast majority of us, it's a grind.

You might wonder why even bother if it doesn't sell any books? The best analogy goes like this:

How do you eat an elephant?

Looking at the next five years, you might feel overwhelmed having to slug out tons of interviews just to sell a few books. Sadly, it's part of the process of getting your name out there. Try to do interviews. Rather than trying to do a ton of appearances all at once, do some slowly over the long term.

Imagine if you did one appearance per week for one year. You will have fifty-two different contact points where strangers acclimated to who you are and what you do. Now, add up fifty-two weeks over the next five years, and you've got 260 different contact points. Wow! So...

> How do you eat an elephant? One bite at a time!

It's not sexy, and it doesn't make for the best plan in getting rich quick. Still, it certainly beats the alternative of investing thousands of dollars into ads that may or may not perform the way you like. Let's face it; you can control elements when landing media appearances. You can answer questions in a live interview or write a guest blog post for a website. You can't control paid advertising as well. There are so many intricate elements involved, not to mention the volatility of advertising if you're new to the game.

Media appearances require much less money and a little more time to get going. If you have more time than money, then landing media appearances is for you. The good news is if you already have a press kit, then you've already done a fair chunk of the work. Now, it's a case of sticking your neck out in a few places and seeing if you can get things going.

Where do you start, and what are the best opportunities out there? Here's a short list to consider for media appearances:

- Local television
- YouTube video interviews
- Podcast interviews
- Local libraries

- In-store appearances

- Guest blog posts

Local Television Appearances

I'll make no qualms in sharing that I've yet to make a single television appearance outside of my time in professional wrestling. It's not an area I actively pursue since my wheelhouse is in online appearances; however, I know my share of authors who have this nailed. The steps are fairly simple in landing a local television appearance.

It may not seem very savvy or as detailed as you would think, but it consists of asking. Call your local TV station and see who you have to speak to for sharing your area of expertise. Make sure you're framing it in a way that makes sense for them while showcasing your expertise as an author. A publicist for traditional publishing authors, Jason Jones, covers the exact steps you'll want to do to land appearances. Rather than misleading you, I'll send you his way so you can nail it every time. Check the resources in the back.

Written Media Appearances

Also, I discovered a really neat resource while reading a book by Honoree Corder. She recommended a news aggregate source called Help a Reporter Out. Also known as HARO, this email newsletter sends out an email three times a day with various news sources looking for specific types of content. The biggest issue is you'll have to do a lot of sifting to find a piece that fits. The easiest way to get to what you're looking for is by using a quick keyword search. Press **CTRL, F**, then type a keyword in the search bar on my computer. If it pulls up any results, then you can skip right to it. If you get no results, then simply toss out the email.

The key with HARO is getting on top of the opportunities right away. Some news sources look immediately for content, so you can't put a pin in it and hope to come back to it later. Typically, I'll let my emails pile up for one day, and then access them the next day. That way, I can peel through each email fast.

Next, you'll have to reach out to the listed contact on HARO and stay on the topic according to their request. Be brief, remain professional, and be ready for rejection. That rejection comes by way of hearing nothing at all or getting a rejection. In most instances, you'll get silence.

This situation is where having your press kit readily available comes in handy. If you spend a little time every day on HARO, you just might get an opportunity in due time. Take note of how you communicated and even ask the reporter what interested them most after fulfilling the commitment.

Online Author Interviews

This is my wheelhouse and an area I can confidently point you. If you're the type of person who doesn't want to be bothered with leaving your house, this option is for you. As long as you have an internet connection, a camera, and a microphone, you're good to go!

You aren't merely limited to any one avenue. Author interviews come in a few different formats, including:

- Video interviews

- Podcast interviews

- Website Interviews

Video Interviews

As shared previously, video marketing should be an integral part of any marketing plan. The nice thing is that even if you're strapped for time and don't have all the resources, you can always rely on someone else to do it all for you. Here is where online author interviews come in. How you land a video interview can be somewhat tricky and a bit time-consuming.

Remember how I had you set up all those social media accounts? It's now time to put them to work. Go to your preferred social media platform where video is available (i.e., YouTube, Facebook, Instagram). Search for content relevant to your niche. You want to scope out video content creators who specifically do interviews on their channel. Though it won't hurt to check out other creators, we want to zero in on video creators who interview guests.

Now comes the grind. You must watch the content. No, you don't have to view twelve hours of video content, but it's a good idea to see if you like the person's content. Otherwise, landing an interview on that channel will be an uphill battle with a terrible payoff. You need to first resonate with the content before ever considering a guest spot with the video creator.

Next, you'll want to engage in the comments with the community. Don't force it and avoid shamelessly self-promoting. Even indirect plugs will get you a side look if you aren't careful. That means, "I just got done writing my book called *XYZ*, and boy, am I tired."

Nope! That indirect promotion will often immediately flag you as someone with an agenda. Keep the comments and communication professional while on-topic. If someone asks you about your content, then be brief and steer the conversation back on-topic. Your primary focus is to be visible and make friends. Become part of the community and engage in meaningful ways.

You don't need to spend the next five years doing this. Still, it's generally a good idea to hang around for a couple of weeks before assaulting the video creator with your proposition. That is where many authors and entrepreneurs get it wrong with me when wanting to land an interview. I turn down more interviews than I accept because some people are not active in my community. None of my followers are invested in the guest and care less about who they are. I'm more apt to work with someone my community already knows, likes, and trusts.

Take your time, and don't rush this step. You'll know when it's the right time to take the next step. Often, a video creator will openly engage with you and even share how much they appreciate your contributions. Don't wait for an invitation to the next step.

You'll need to do a little recon once you feel comfortable with the video creator's content. Look up their website, social media account, or any of their profiles. You're looking for an email or contact form. Once you find it, reach out to them, but keep it brief. Bear in mind, video creators are busy, and answering every last message becomes an exhausting process, so keep it short. For example:

Hey, Dale,

I've enjoyed your YouTube channel for the past few weeks.

You may have noticed me in the comments from time to time.

I loved your interview with Dave Chesson; it was highly informative.

I'm reaching out to you to see how I could get an interview on your channel.

I'm a self-published author who grew an advanced reader copy team to over 1000 members in the past 90 days.

I believe your audience will love some of the insights I have.

Also, I will promote my appearance through my email list and Twitter for the next few weeks.

Thoughts?

Before you consider typing that out word for word, I encourage you to write your own. It doesn't need to be perfect. In fact, don't make it a form letter. Trust me, video creators get a ton of queries, and we know when someone has merely copied and pasted some form letter. It took me two minutes to write. It should take you the same amount of time, especially if you already know, like, and trust the creator.

Four elements to consider when approaching a video creator for an interview are:

1. **Confirmation** — Tell the creator about how you know them. Don't go over the top.

2. **Compliment** — Okay, I'm not asking you to kiss their ass, but it's a good idea to tell them why you dig their content. It could be a specific video or two, or you can even refer to something unique to the community.

3. **Deliver value** — How can you be of service to the creator's community? Most video creators want to know you have their community's best interests at heart.

4. **Quid pro quo** — Remember, you're dipping into somebody else's community they have taken the time to grow and nurture. Not

1. to mention, the video creator will have to work to put your interview together and promote it to their following. What's in it for them? No matter how big or small, explain to them how you plan to promote it and what audience you'll bring to the table.

If a video creator accepts your offer, honor their time by asking for a scheduling app if they have it. If they don't, be prepared to do a little schedule tag with them to make it work. I'd recommend getting a scheduling app that integrates with your preferred online calendar. Then, you can always save heartache for both of you and drop a link to it.

Remember the press kit I had you put together? It's time to put that to use. Once you get booked for a video interview, give them the press kit. Do not wait for them to ask for it. A prepared guest leaves an excellent first impression, so send that press kit right after they agree to have you on their show.

Now, find out the answer to these questions:

1. Where do you need to be?

2. What do you need for the interview?

3. How long will the interview be?

4. What expectations do they have of you?

5. Are you able to share your book and relevant links?

For any interview, I'd recommend having everything set up well in advance. Make sure wherever you plan to conduct the interview (i.e., your house, office, etc.), your background is clutter and distraction-free. No cringe-inducing virtual greenscreens! It's an awful look and will hinder more than help you. Clean up your area for the interview and be done with it.

Also, test your computer on a video chat ahead of time. Reach out to a friend and see if they'll do a video with you. Heck, it might even be a good time for you first-timers to do a mock interview. It will break up your nerves and get you relaxed for the actual interview. Watch out for glitchy video, choppy audio, or any imperfections that'll take away from your spotlight.

There are two things you must not do without in video interviews:

1. Headphones to isolate sound and avoid echoes.

2. Direct internet access — do not rely on WiFi. Avoid it at all costs. Only use WiFi if you must. It's a good idea to fully disclose with your host that you have to rely on WiFi (if you do).

Once the day comes, loosen up and have fun. After the interview, take a moment to thank the host. Do not disconnect right away, because sometimes the host might have additional points to communicate. In some instances, they might have special thanks or compliments.

Send a follow-up email thanking them for the interview. A little goes a long way. As a video creator, I'm more apt to bring someone back who was not only a good guest but went the extra distance to say thanks while promoting the content. Speaking of content, find out the interview link so you can uphold your end of the deal for promotion.

Podcast Interviews

Audio blew up big time over the past few years. Between podcasts and downloadable audiobooks, more people gravitate toward audio than ever before. Why? It's easily consumable information, you don't need much of an internet connection to listen, and it's highly accessible and portable content. Getting podcast interviews is a solid win for building awareness of your author brand.

Podcasts work much in the same way video interviews do. Most of the time, you won't even need video. Everything you did for preparation in the video arena, you can now do with audio. Before you do solicit an interview, double-check the host. Some podcasts do audio and video. You don't want to show up on the day of your interview to find out you needed your webcam on. Worse yet, imagine showing up in nothing but your underwear only to find you need to be on-camera.

I've found podcast interviews to be the easiest to land. No matter how big or small, give a podcast a shot. Don't make the same mistake I made. Quite a few times, I accepted interviews without first listening to the podcast, and it's been a comedy of errors. Some hosts are hard to understand due to thick accents or bad audio gear. Other times, the host seems more interested in pushing their content versus interviewing me.

On one podcast, I had the host do an entire intro and talk for quite a while before she ever got to me. Once the host did ask me questions, she interrupted me mid-sentence to interject her thoughts. At the end of the interview, the host wanted me to ask her questions. Yep, you didn't read that wrong; the host wanted me to interview her on *her* show. After twenty minutes of this train wreck of a podcast, I was ready to crawl in a hole and cry myself to sleep. She seemed to love my interview. I listened back and discovered it was as bad as I thought it would be. Sadly, she wanted me back, and I had to politely decline.

The moral of the story is to never accept a podcast booking without first knowing the type of content and how the host conducts the show. Had I listened to the offending podcaster's content, I would have discovered she had a history of mistreating her guests.

After any interview, whether audio or video, ask how the host felt about your performance. You aren't fishing for compliments so much as you're setting yourself up for future interviews. If the host enjoyed your content, ask them if they know of any other platforms where you can get interviews. This is a great way to get referrals! I've had some guests on my channel who knocked the ball out of the park, so I referred them to other peers in my industry. In turn, that guest got more bookings!

If your interview was horrible (and you'll know), don't approach the host about referrals. It's generally not a good look. Again, you'll know whether you did well or not. It's a gut feeling.

For getting podcast interviews, you jump through the same hoops as finding the various platforms relevant to your niche. I don't necessarily feel you should pay an exorbitant fee to a podcasting interview curation service. It's ridiculous that someone would charge a client hundreds of dollars to get on a podcast when all you have to do is lay the groundwork and do the outreach and show up.

A good free service is through a website called PodcastGuests.com. Though they have a premium service for hosting guest profiles, you'll get your money's worth through the free service alone. Every week, PodcastGuests.com sends out an email showcasing podcast guests and podcasts looking for guests. I easily landed a dozen interviews and developed long-lasting relationships with podcasters using this free service. Not every newsletter will bring back something for you, but if you keep an eye on it, it will pay off.

Website Interviews

Getting website interviews is possibly the easiest way while showcasing your skills as a writer. I tripped over this option quite some time ago when first getting into the business. How it works is the website has a form you fill out. You answer questions based on your experience and submit all your relevant information. The website then showcases you in the online interview.

It's a nice way to share who you are in a different place than your website or Amazon. The best part is this option comes 100% free. I've never found a site that charges for it. One site that's a great example of website interviews is AwesomeGang.com. It'll take you about fifteen to twenty minutes to complete.

If you're wondering where else to find author interviews like this, I'd recommend looking into promotional websites. Most want you to complete an interview because it helps them build more relevancy in search engines, especially if you send traffic to read your interview. You'd be doing yourself a great service by promoting your interview after the site posts it.

Local libraries

Not too long ago, my wife and I attended the Dayton Book Expo. We saw many great exhibitors and authors at the conference and were pleasantly surprised by a panel of guest experts. These folks were on the inside when it comes to leveraging libraries for your author brand. I never thought about working with local libraries, and according to the panelists, it is a highly untapped market.

You would be surprised to know local libraries are looking for home-grown authors to showcase in the community. The only catch is you have to be willing to put in the work and build relationships with the library staff.

Do you want to get your book into the local library? Then, speak to the branch library manager. Don't just assault them with your books and leave. You need to be willing to invest a bit more time and value to get something in return from the library. You might want to volunteer time, organize a book club, or run a workshop based on your niche at the library. All it takes is speaking with the library staff and see what you can do to help.

Landing a library speaking gig is as simple as stepping outside your comfort zone and speaking with the staff. I spoke with one panelist about her extensive experience in working with libraries. She assured me all it requires is a little time, research, and work to build a relationship with the libraries. After giving back to your community, they're more apt to have you make appearances and promote those appearances.

In-Store Appearances

Much like libraries, landing in-store appearances requires a little upfront work and patience. You'll need to visit the local bookstores and let them know who you are and what you do. Sadly, most brick and mortar stores aren't looking for volunteers. Still, if you're a regular patron who chops it up with the staff, then they'll be more receptive when you pitch an in-store appearance. The most important thing when it comes to landing an in-store appearance is WIIFT – what's in it for them?

I hate to say this, and it's not to discourage you, but authors are a dime a dozen. What do you bring to the table that all the others don't? How do you plan to advertise the appearance? What kind of foot traffic will you bring?

There's nothing sadder than the lonely author sitting at their booth in the local mom and pop bookstore. If there's no one visiting, what do you think the initial reaction will be for people? It will most likely be a dismissive reaction, or in some cases, the author might appear to be a store worker.

I'd recommend before you pitch a local store about an in-store appearance, have a strategy in place. What will you do that isn't just about signing books and kissing babies? How will you make this a memorable event? Consider developing creative out-of-the-box ideas. Instead of doing autograph sessions, maybe consider doing a read-along, a workshop, or a Q&A session. There are no limitations.

Remember to go in with a pitch that isn't just, "Hi, I'm a local author. You should host an author signing because I'm going to be big."

That won't cut the mustard, and most people will pass.

A long time ago, I was a reckless driver who had no common sense or driver's etiquette. Heck, I was so arrogant, I believed having an insurance policy was for suckers. Despite it being an Ohio mandate, I still didn't have insurance. Inevitably, I got in a wreck. Yes, it was 100% my fault. To spare you the details, I gently t-boned a car I didn't see while making a left turn in a parking lot. Thankfully, no one was hurt, but my bank account would be when it was all said and done.

Even though I hardly tapped the other car, it was enough to do damage. It was hundreds of dollars I couldn't afford. I could have avoided all of that had I shelved my ego and invested in a good insurance policy. The accident was enough to humble me, and I never did it again.

There are real-world examples in self-publishing of authors who've been just as reckless with their business. They rely solely on Amazon to build their business. These authors can pull in a substantial income only for Amazon to shut them out. The fact is, Amazon doesn't need to have a reason to terminate accounts. It's their sandbox; we're merely playing in it.

What happens when Amazon kicks you off their platform? Do you simply tuck tail and go away, or do you fight back and reinstate your account? Can't you just start a new account with a different business entity? Well, that's certainly debatable and nothing I'd recommend.

If Amazon boots you off their platform, then it's up to you to pick up the pieces and make the most of the situation.

Author terminations on the Amazon platform don't happen often, but it's still a real possibility. Much like my chances of getting into a car accident didn't seem likely, it still happened, nonetheless. Rather than thinking, "it won't happen to me," you should always prepare for the worst while expecting the best. Enter email marketing.

Email marketing is your insurance policy. The fact of the matter is Amazon has customers. You're using Amazon's platform to reach their customers. Once Amazon banishes you, you can't take the customers with you, or can you?

Well, there's a good reason why email marketing is your safeguard. By having readers join an email list, you convert Amazon customers into your followers. Once they join your email list, you have essentially brought your following with you. Now, would you have the same reach as you do on Amazon? No, but something is better than nothing. You can build a presence online through avenues like social media or a website. However, nothing compares to the relationships you create through the email inbox.

I purposely saved email marketing for the end of the book. Without any of the previous suggestions, building an email list will be an uphill battle. To get the most from building an email following, it's a good idea to:

1. Have a website.

2. Build a presence on social media.

3. Publish or plan to publish a book.

1. Understand basic marketing and promotion.

Getting someone to trust you enough to part ways with their email address is a tight rope walk. On the one hand, you've got to deliver value for them to trust you enough. On the other hand, if you over-deliver, potential subscribers will see you as a try-hard or someone who's simply in it to sell things. Sure, you want to deliver value, but in the same instance, you don't want to go overboard and scare people away. Part of that is understanding what your audience wants before ever starting an email list.

What is the Best Email Marketing Service?

Before you start gathering emails and blindly sending them out through your Hotmail account, you need to understand a few things. Never under any circumstance, do email marketing through a regular email account. It's a surefire way to get marked as spam and blacklisted online. Next, you should never send content without consent from the email recipient. You can't prove whether they consented if you simply add their email to your list. They need to opt into your email newsletter, not you. Last, you need to get a good overhead view of what email marketing is and how to leverage it.

The best place to start when it comes to email marketing is through an email service provider. You've got a ton of services to choose including:

- Mailchimp
- MailerLite
- ConvertKit
- GetResponse

- Aweber

- Infusionsoft

- And, so much more

Rather than point you to one over the other, I'll leave it up to you to research your options. If you're new to self-publishing, I'd recommend considering any service that'll allow you free services with a cap or a trial. Keep in mind, sometimes free services come with limitations, but you'll at least have an option you can use until you get the hang of email marketing.

Some services like Mailchimp and MailerLite allow up to 1000 subscribers for free. Once you have that many subscribers, you should have a good sense of monetizing your email list. You can do that by sending unique offers, announce book launches, or even build up awareness of your existing catalog.

Ask around in your community and see what your peers prefer. Take any recommendations with a grain of salt. At the end of the day, you're going to be the person in charge of email marketing, not them. If you are using an email service provider with astronomical rates, that's on you, not your friend, who recommended it to you.

Once you set up your service, you'll need to get familiar with all the tools and functions. Since all platforms have different layouts, I'll skip telling you how to get them set up. Ask yourself these questions:

- Can readers easily join the email list?

- Are the metrics easily accessible?

- What do you have to pay based on the number of subscribers and outbound emails?

In 2015, I joined several Facebook groups with successful self-publishers. Quite a few of them had me believe my email marketing efforts were futile. After all, they boasted hundreds of thousands of subscribers, and here I was with a whopping one hundred. It was rather frustrating, to say the least. What I came to understand was that the people who flexed their subscriber base were most often the ones who did nothing with that list.

They hadn't sent a single email broadcast to their subscribers. That means they didn't even give their subscribers a reason to unsubscribe. These try-hards were so busy bragging about their large base they forgot to communicate with them altogether. That's the most critical aspect of building your list. Whether big or small, always communicate regularly with your subscribers.

Understanding the Email Metrics

The point of building a list is to communicate with your audience and nurture a long-lasting relationship. Furthermore, you're building an email list so that you can sell more books, products, or services as an author. Before you can ever expect to sell anything, you need to understand what numbers are important.

With any email service provider (ESP), you will need to track opens and clicks. How many people received your email? How many of those recipients opened the email? Of those emails opened, how many people clicked on a link or offer?

Yes, having a deep list of subscribers is great, but if no one is opening your email, you've got a problem. The first barrier of entry when it comes to mastering email marketing is the subject line. You need to compel an email subscriber to open your email. That requires a bit of copywriting finesse. If you aren't good at it, don't sweat it. You can always experiment with different titles and subject lines to see what gets the best results. Some ESPs allow for split testing to try a different subject line for two groups of email subscribers. Once you find a good subject line, you can use it again or tweak it for future campaigns.

After you get the email subscriber to open your email, the next mission is to deliver value. Create an email worth reading; otherwise, they will unsubscribe or tune out all future emails. Rather than writing long-form emails, go into it with a game plan with short-form ad copy. Create a concise email with the intent to drive the traffic elsewhere. How do you do that? Simply through a link.

That brings us to the second most important metric – clicks. Where email opens get someone into your newsletter, the click sends them out of their inbox and into the online ethos. You could send them to your social media profile, a blog article, or even your latest book. The hard part is figuring out how you do it. No, you don't need special neurolinguistic programming skills or Jedi mind tricks. Again, it comes down to delivering enough value and building enough intrigue to merit a visit to your link.

After that, all bets are off. What happens next will depend largely on where you're sending them—some ESPs track sales for some sites. Sadly, there isn't any ESP who integrates with Amazon, so you won't be able to know who bought your book. That's including the use of Amazon Associates. Sadly, it's against Amazon Associates' policies to use affiliate links in emails. Instead, send email subscribers to your website since you can embed offers there.

Closely monitor how many subscribers you have, how many open your emails, and how many are clicking your links. The rest will fall into place as it should. Check the resources section for my recommended reads on email marketing. Rather than spend a lot of time lingering on email marketing, let's focus on how to get email subscribers?

How to Build an Email List

Getting an email subscriber isn't easy, but the process can be simple. Once you settle on an email service provider, you should be able to build a landing page. Most ESPs have the option to build a webpage specifically for subscribing to your newsletter. This is called a landing page or squeeze page. Most landing pages consist of a simple graphic, some ad copy, one or two text boxes for the person's name and email, and an opt-in button.

Once you create a landing page, get the URL associated with the landing page. The first thing you should do is create a short link, sub-domain, or subdirectory as a redirect. It's hard enough to ask readers to subscribe to you. Imagine how much more of an ask it is for you to require them to remember or trust a random website link.

One additional item to consider is the lead magnet, a special bonus that entices people to join your email list. Is a lead magnet required? No, but it certainly helps attract more subscribers than if you offer nothing. There's something to be said, though, about the people who subscribed with no real bribe. I've found email lists where I had no offer have the greatest open and click rate. Why? Possibly because those subscribers are more invested and loyal to my author brand and didn't need any coaxing to get onboard.

The best-performing lead magnets are sometimes the simplest to create. Don't go overboard and test out a few different lead magnets over time. Once you find an irresistible offer, drive more traffic to it. A few examples of some lead magnets you can create are:

1. **Fiction** — short story or novella — don't give away everything as a fiction author. Think about building a prequel or spinoff to your flagship books.

2. **Nonfiction** — checklist, toolkit, or mini-course — as a nonfiction author, all three perform well. In my experience, checklists and toolkits perform the best. Keep it to one page. You can even use the ever-reliable Canva to create a robust PDF download for your subscribers.

Once you have a great lead magnet, you can host it on your ESP or in the cloud. I've had quite a few files hosted in the free Google Drive service associated with my private email. I simply grab a shareable link, then paste the link in the welcome email. Once someone subscribes, the first email is the welcome email with instructions on downloading their free offer. Don't be surprised when you see this email gets the most opens and clicks. The second email or so tend to get the most unsubscribes. That's okay! That just means you can communicate directly with the people who are genuinely interested in you as an author.

The next step is to promote your landing page. You'll want to plaster this web address anywhere and everywhere, including:

- Books

- Video mentions and descriptions

- During interviews

- Your social media profile or feed

- Guest blog posts

When it comes to books, you'll want to insert the offer to join your email list in two high traffic areas – in your front matter and back matter. Anyone browsing the Amazon marketplace can see the first 10% of your book. Part of that first 10% could include a one-page mention of your email newsletter. You can keep it simple with something like:

> Would you like to get exclusive offers, free advanced copies, and special discounts on books by this author? Then, subscribe at XYZ.com to join our email reader club.

Though this isn't the most effective ad copy out there, it's roped me in a few hundred subscribers in any given year. Just imagine if I added an offer they couldn't refuse. Try this:

> Wanna know the secret to sell more books with only a few minor tweaks in your publishing process? Then, download a copy of the Bestseller Book Launch Checklist today when you join the VIP Readers Club at DaleLinks.com/Checklist.

The only wrong way to build an email list is if you outright lie to get them on your list. Avoid roping in unsuspecting subscribers with outrageous claims or unrealistic promises. If you're promising to deliver three epic-length novels, then you better deliver, or you are going to have many unhappy subscribers and an eroded reputation.

Building an Advanced Reader Copy Team

To set your next publication up for the best possible success, you need to get enough hype behind the launch. Though the email list is a great place to tap into, you're going to need a narrower subset of people.

These are readers who enjoy your content and are willing to provide reviews upon launching. Enter the advanced reader copy team, also known as an ARC team.

Before you launch a book to the public, it's a good idea to build hype in your community. You can further build hype by opening up free, yet limited, access to your book to a select number of readers. The best way to find an ARC reader is through your email newsletter. You can send out a handful of emails searching for subscribers who are the most interested in receiving an advanced copy.

To make it even easier on yourself, you can simply narrow your audience in your ESP dashboard. Find out who your most engaged users are. Once you identify the group of super active subscribers, you're going to send them an exclusive offer to join your advanced reader copy team.

The ARC team members' only responsibilities are to read the book and send any feedback to you before it launches. Once the book launches, they post a review on Amazon, Goodreads, or any other platform you wish. Remember, you can't require leaving a review of your book. Amazon Community Guidelines forbid coercion or review exchanges. You can only request that they leave an honest review once the book launches. That's it.

In my Bestseller Book Launch Checklist (available at DaleLinks.com/ Checklist), one of the first, most vital steps to a stellar book launch is assembling an ARC team. One of the next steps is to create a preorder followed by launching the print version of the book two weeks before the ebook launch. This release strategy allows for your ARC readers to post a review on the book before the full release of the ebook. Having reviews before the launch, you build more relevancy for your book and assist browsing customers in making an informed purchase.

Just how many members do you need on your ARC team? That largely depends on how many free copies you want to distribute. If some of your followers already read your book, then how likely are they to purchase a copy post-launch? Possibly not very likely, but it's a chance worth taking if you can get reviews on your book.

I found an ARC team is great in theory, but in practice, it doesn't always play out as planned. For instance, you might have ten members on your ARC team, but only three people post a review after launch. This means you have a 30% conversion rate of readers to reviewers. This is an actual number I had at one point. Rather than face having only three reviews on launch day, I tripled the number of team members. When I had thirty members on my ARC team, I received ten reviews post-launch. Do you see how that works? It's a numbers game. If you've done a good job in delivering a stellar publication and communicating your needs, then your ARC readers should deliver when the time is right.

I find following up with ARC team members before launch is critical. I check in to see how the reading is coming. Then, I send out an email a week before the launch, and I do it one more time on the day of the launch. If you find some ARC members are dragging their feet, follow up with them about one to four weeks after launch. Beyond that, if your ARC member isn't reading the book or posting a review, simply remove them from the team and move on.

Back in the day, I uploaded all my ebook files (epub, mobi, and PDF) to a cloud drive. Now, there are a ton of services that'll do it for you. Some services will even watermark your files and only allow for downloads after a reader jumps through some hoops to get on your ARC team. Services like BookFunnel, BookSprout, Prolific Works, and Hidden Gems Books are examples of premium sites that help with file management and gathering ARC team members.

If you're a bit more cash-strapped and want free alternatives, look into StoryOrigin or FiveABook. Both services are new on the market and are currently offering free submissions. They have a variety of services available beyond ARC building features. The one I worked with on the previous book in this series, *Amazon Keywords for Books*, was StoryOrigin. The user interface is intuitive, and the process of accepting ARC readers is stress-free.

All I had to do was upload the ebook in three formats under 7MB and three sample versions of each file type. If you're having issues with getting the various file types or compressing your files, the team at StoryOrigin has you covered with video tutorials. I also needed to upload all my book's metadata, including the title, subtitle, author name, book description, and book cover. Once I had all the content uploaded, I selected my preferred platform for my reviews.

The rest was up to me. I had to share it with my following and invite my email subscribers to join the ARC team. When people came into request access, I could accept or reject them based on their posts and their prior experience on various platforms. The nice part is StoryOrigin asks the reader for their Amazon reviewer profile so I could get an idea of their review history.

After my book launched, I sent a notification with an Amazon link for all of my ARC readers to leave a review. StoryOrigin makes life easy, and the best part is, it's completely affordable for all self-publishers.

I'd be remiss if I didn't mention one key area StoryOrigin has dialed in – newsletter swaps. You're able to collaborate with other authors in or around your genre through your email list. If you have a book or ARC you want to promote, you can have another author share it with their email newsletter. In return, you promote one of their products. The best part is you can see what the other author wants you to promote long before you agree to do the newsletter swap.

Newsletter swaps are a great way to work with other authors to raise brand awareness. You're able to cross-pollinate and grow your respective lists. If you lack content to send out to subscribers, then newsletter swaps are an easy way to provide continued value to your list. Just be selective about who you align with for this purpose. Always double-check their content and make sure it makes sense to promote it.

For instance, I have no issue with doing a newsletter swap, but you won't find me working with fiction authors for my nonfiction brand devoted to self-publishing. I can't justify the promotion, and it will confuse my subscribers. I don't want to erode the trust of my subscribers or irritate them with irrelevant offers. Also, I'm selective with how many swaps I do. I don't want to overwhelm myself with the extra work or turn off my readers because that's all I'm doing is promoting everyone else.

When building out your email list, growing your ARC team, and collaborating with other authors, remember why you're doing it in the first place – the reader. If you never lose sight of why you want to build an email list in the first place, you'll never go wrong. You should build an email list as a way to connect with your readers. If ever the day comes when you no longer use or require Amazon for your author brand, then at least you took your audience with you.

*A*dmittedly, I saved the best for last. It's a huge topic you shouldn't take lightly - networking. I believe networking is the most underutilized tool in marketing and promotion for books. Quite a few authors are known for being reclusive and introverted, hidden away from the world. The biggest problem lies therein. How can you even begin to expect people to find your books, much less, discover who you are if you're in some shack that's miles off the grid?

Ever hear the phrase:

> It's all about who you know.

That's not just some cheeky phrase or a line concocted by a crazed conspiracy theorist. It's the actual truth. The more people you know and have in your network, the more avenues open up to you as an author. The issues are:

1. Where do you begin?
2. Who do you talk to?
3. How does networking work?
4. How does it serve your author brand?

I was reluctant to break into this topic because a single chapter couldn't begin to cover what I learned through decades of experience in networking. I'll do my best to give you a few highlights and tips to get you started on the right foot. That way, you can build a network of business professionals on which you can rely.

Simply put, networking is when you create a group of acquaintances and associates. To keep your network active, you'll need to communicate regularly. It seems rather daunting at first, but it's much the same as writing an epic novel. It's never a good idea to write an 80,000-word or longer manuscript in one sitting. Instead, you should slowly chip away at crafting your book, one day at a time with one micro-step per movement. Building out your network isn't something that will happen overnight or through one business meeting. It takes plenty of interactions before you can lean on a business professional to be in your network.

Before you go to a Chamber of Commerce meeting or join a local meetup, you need to get a basic understanding of etiquette while networking. I've been to hundreds of meetings, and I can assure you, many business professionals get it wrong. The bad example is usually the blowhard, ego-centric entrepreneur who's there for the food while littering his business card everywhere. A good example is easier than you know. If you skip this chapter, then at least remember this little set of rules:

1. Ask questions.

2. Be approachable.

3. Try to make a new friend.

4. Listen more than you talk.

5. Offer your contact info only when asked.

These rules apply to all walks, whether you're doing in-person events or online virtual meetups. It requires no work whatsoever, and people will appreciate you for it.

People love to know when you hear them, so it's no surprise that people love to answer questions, especially when it's about them or their business. One of the easiest icebreakers for networking is just to introduce yourself and immediately ask their name. Follow it up by asking what they do for a living and for how long. That's enough to grease the wheels on the conversation. Don't stop asking questions. I challenge myself never to tell the other person my profession until they nearly demand to know what I do. Why? Again, people love to talk about themselves and their business. Since you already know what you're all about, what's the point in sharing it? So, you can hear it out loud? People truly don't care what you know until they know that you actually care.

Don't just ask questions to fill dead air. Show genuine interest in the other person. It might be a stretch at first, but everyone has common ground. If you ask enough questions, you'll find that common ground.

If you're an introvert like me, then it might be your first inclination to be a wallflower at networking events. That's okay as long as you don't wait until the last minute to act. The easiest way to warm up is to go directly to the first person you see and start a conversation. It sucks at first and sometimes feels incredibly awkward, but once you talk to one person, it's much easier to talk to others.

If you're not the type of person to start a conversation, at least remain approachable. That means you put your cellphone down for a minute. It's a crutch anyway. Open yourself up and make eye contact with other people. I promise it won't hurt to put on a smile. It doesn't need to be cheesy or over the top. Just give people a slight inclination that you won't bite if they approach you.

At social events, avoid hovering around the food or drinks table. You might as well be buried nose deep in your phone. Though the food is there for consumption, it can be a crutch and prevent you from chatting with everyone. I typically stuff my face full before I go to an event, so the only thing I need is a bottle of water when I arrive. The worst type of conversation is when you start chatting about the food or catering. Nope! The food isn't going to be a good common ground. After all, how do you pivot your conversation from the food to your author brand? It's near impossible.

When at business meetups, I try to make a new friend. There's nothing shady about my approach, and I have no ulterior motive. I want to find someone with whom I can connect. Not just on a business level, but on a personal level too. Do I count them out if we don't click on a visceral level? No, but it certainly helps to build a connection that's deeper and more meaningful beyond business.

The biggest mistake I see many people making at these types of meetings is talking too much. Don't get me wrong, you should talk, but know how to read the room. Share only enough to get the conversation going. If you find the conversation dying down, you can fire things back up with a thought-provoking question. When I recommend listening more than you talk, I don't insinuate you sit on your thumbs and wait your turn. You just have to find a balance between motormouth and wallflower.

The last rule I gave was to offer your contact info only when asked. Should you go to a business meeting with cards? Absolutely! Is it required? No. Because if you're making meaningful connections with other business professionals, then chances are likely, they won't need cardstock with your information on it. If you made enough of a good impression, they'll remember you and go searching for your contact.

One of my favorite things to do is go to a business meeting without a business card. Yes, I do it purposely. It forces me to be proactive in my conversations. The first thing I do when asked for a business card is to tell them I don't have any, but I have them pull out their phone and dial in my website, YouTube channel, or Amazon profile page. They'll most likely glance at it and continue the conversation. Later on, when they go into their phone, they will be reminded of me and our conversation. The nice part is it didn't cost me a dime and functioned better than any business card since it showed them my brand instead of some general contact info.

If you do have business cards, only take about half a dozen with you to meetings. That way, it forces you to be selective with who gets your card. There's nothing worse than leaving a meeting and seeing your cards littered all over the place. Mitigate this issue by handing out far less.

Speaking of business cards, what do you do with them? For me, I rarely hold onto a business card. It's clutter, and I have no use for them if I use a simple strategy. The day after a meeting, follow up with the person who handed you the business card. Send an email or call them. It doesn't need to be anything fancy and depends mostly on what you chatted about at your meeting. The simple act of follow-up is one that has left an indelible impression on my network. If I don't have a lot of time, I take a picture of the card and toss it out. I always include a follow-up sequence, so I stay in front-of-mind of my network.

I met a good friend, Melina Shah, at a local Chamber of Commerce meeting. We hit it off from the get-go and have kept loose contact with each other over the years. Melina used to use an app that scanned business cards. The app would store all the important data and then place the business professional into a contact sequence. She would get little reminders to reach out to the person. Also, Melina had someone in her contact list who would be of help when she needed it.

One of the things you should not do is enter a conversation with the sole intent of pushing your agenda. I used to work with a guy in network marketing who was the next level of creepy. This guy would go to grocery stores with zero intention of buying food. His only intent was to meet people and try to push his multi-level marketing (MLM) products on them. It was predatory and off-putting.

Do not get into networking if your sole intent is to push your agenda. When you show people you care, they'll become your biggest cheer-leader, but when you show people you only care for yourself, you won't make many friends.

That's the whole thing around networking – building a network of friends and acquaintances you can lean on. That way, when it comes time for you to get help on your next launch, you can call on them. When you need help with a specific aspect of your business, you can call on someone. When you are stuck and don't know a way out, you can call on your network.

Where exactly do you find places to network? There's an unending supply of places to check out. Here are a few:

- **Local meetups** – Check your local Chamber of Commerce, Meetup.com, or local Facebook Groups.

- **Social Media Outreach** – Be tasteful and selective with how you approach people on social media. Don't be that weird guy spamming people's LinkedIn direct messages. Treat any virtual

- meeting like an in-person meeting. Follow the same rules as mentioned previously.

- **Online Virtual Meetings and Conferences** — Again, you can find these types of gatherings through Meetup.com or local Facebook Groups. Ask around, and you might find more.

- **In-Person Conferences** – This is, by far, the most beneficial of all the ways I network. When someone is willing to invest in an in-person conference, they're extremely motivated to elevate their business. Also, you have a common ground, so the ice-breaker conversation is way easier.

If you're feeling somewhat overwhelmed at the prospect of networking, it's okay. Everyone has been there. Don't let my little rules limit you. It's okay if you stumble because you can always dust yourself off and get back at it again. The most important thing to do when it comes to networking is – just do it. It's better you try than make no effort at all. You're only one contact away from extending your reach and exploding your author platform.

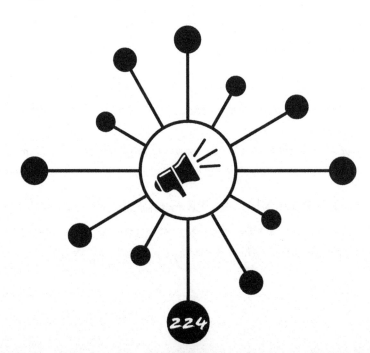

224

*G*etting reviews for your book should be an integral part of your marketing and promotion plan. Though some would-be experts would have you believe getting a certain number of reviews is the trick to gaining the favor of Amazon, that isn't necessarily true. As shared in my book *Amazon Keywords for Books*, reviews play a small part in building relevance for your title in the Amazon algorithm. Still, the results are fleeting and don't last.

What does last is the impression a reader makes when posting a review of your book on the Amazon platform. It's the catchy buzzword people throw around called "social proof." Don't let the buzzword fool you; it's a fancy way of saying you got third-party credibility. By having a reader post their candid thoughts of your work, more potential readers can make an informed purchase when they come across your book on Amazon.

Can you sell books without having any reviews? Sure! I've sold hundreds of books with no reviews. Can you imagine how many more I would've sold had I gotten a few more people to post their honest insights?

Reviews reveal the experience the buyer had to the browsing customer. Whether perceived as good or bad, a review tells a story about your book. That story can be one that informs a potential reader about how they might enjoy your work. Remember, even when you get a low scoring review, those can also be beneficial to the growth of your book.

Book reviews are a great way to market your product on Amazon better. A book with more reviews appears more attractive than one that doesn't have any. Reviews also play an integral part in your promotion plan because you can share snippets of what readers enjoyed most about your work. Sometimes, a reader says it better than the writer. Rather than trying to come up with the best ad copy, a review snippet will suffice.

Instead of going neck-deep into another topic, I will put a pin in the book reviews topic for the third part in the *Amazon Self Publisher Series, Amazon Reviews for Books*. Getting book reviews is a challenging and often misunderstood part of the self-publishing process. For now, I recommend making review gathering a part of your marketing and promotion strategy. A little goes a long way!

*A*fter my mother left my eighteenth birthday celebration, I knocked on a few doors in my dorm. One person after the other came flocking to gobble down the free bits of leftover cake. Before I knew it, the whole cake was history. None of my newfound friends had any issue with staying and chatting. I came to form some early lifelong bonds with these relative strangers.

The following year, for my nineteenth birthday, I was already living off-campus. After having such a downer of a birthday party, I made sure to hype and promote the heck out of my party. My little two-bedroom apartment was full of people. We didn't eat just cake. Partygoers enjoyed oversized cookies, alcohol, pizza, and a wild assortment of goodies fit for an over-the-top celebration. The people who joined me included all my friends from the dorm. Not a single hometown acquaintance attended that night. Frankly, I didn't miss them. We were having too much fun to miss anyone.

Heck, the party got so loud, and out of hand, even the cops paid us a visit to quiet us down a little. That didn't put a damper on things, and the party continued to run off the rails. My previous birthday party paled in comparison. All it took was a little more hyping, building more relationships, and getting to know what my audience wanted from a party.

What a difference one year makes. I met many new people and made quite a few new friends. They were more than happy to show up. Some of them even came early and never left until the next morning!

That's how your book should be. When you put pen to paper, the world should already know about it. As you churn out chapter after chapter of content, people need to know your book is on its way. Once your book launches, your ideal reader should be feverishly waiting to snatch a copy out of your hands. After the book is out, remind readers often of it being there.

Once you finish having a book that only your mother can be proud of, let's get you to publish a book the whole world can enjoy too. Now, get out there and market your book right and promote it till kingdom come!

AMAZON
REVIEWS
for
BOOKS

HOW TO GET BOOK REVIEWS ON AMAZON

Reviews ▾ | **Contents** | 🔍

I love tacos. There's no way around it. I tried everything I could to avoid eating tacos. Inevitably, my life guides me toward the nearest taco vendor. Any old taco will not do. I need some assurance the tacos are of premium quality and not some low-grade stuff. Price isn't the issue so much as how good the food is and the value of the service. Naturally, I'll dig out my phone and look up reviews on the establishment. I'm always drawn to the low one-star reviews and tend to scan past the high marks and praise in the five-star reviews. I want to see the complaints. It's easy to give a restaurant, service, or product a high review. It's the low reviews that tell a better story.

When I first moved to downtown Columbus, I visited the Condado Tacos restaurant around the corner from my place. I whipped out Yelp, scanned through the low reviews, and found some rather innocuous complaints about lousy service and improper food serving. Beyond that, it seemed good to go. Little did I know that I'd spend thousands of dollars and countless hours visiting this restaurant. To say I'm a fan is a huge understatement. Between birthdays and business meetings, I've done just about everything there is to do at Condado Tacos.

Naturally, any time someone comes into town, I take them to Condado Tacos. If I have a business meeting, then I take them to Condado Tacos. When my wife and I need to get out of the house, we go to Condado Tacos. My enthusiasm for the restaurant spilled so far out of my life;

233

I've seen friends and family even visit when I'm not with them. That speaks volumes about how excellent their service is.

Of course, I left beaming reviews on Yelp and Google. I've checked in through the Yelp app, snapped some pictures, and tagged some friends. In turn, all the people I brought to the establishment did the same. They brought in more friends who became hooked. All those people then left great reviews. I'm sure it had a massive ripple effect throughout the whole Columbus-area.

It all started with reviews. Had I not seen a review about the establishment, I would've been less likely to go in. After all, there's a Chipotle – the McDonald's of Mexican food - not even a mile down the road. I didn't want to experience the same ol' tired taco fanfare. I wanted something a bit different on that given day, and I was not disappointed.

Imagine how different life would be had I not seen some type of social proof. Would I skip the restaurant without some validation? Would I go to Chipotle, where they have countless reviews? Would I be brave enough to give it a shot and try it out? Would the other people who came with me try out the place? Would the people who would have seen my review passed on those tasty tacos? These are what-if scenarios we won't truly know.

The fact is we're in a day and age where social proof is almost a necessity. To cut through the noise, be heard above the pack, and stand out from the rest, we need someone to lend third-party credibility. It's that stamp of approval, or sometimes disapproval, we need to show we have something worth considering.

Self-publishing can be a dark, hard, and lonely road as it is. To make matters worse, we cannot even begin to gain traction without someone saying, "Hey, this author's alright."

Sometimes, it's not enough to even get one person saying it. It's not even a given number of people saying it. We need a consistent stream of social proof to earn the trust of a potential reader. Where one review posted in 2015 was good five years ago, it doesn't speak to your product's relevance today.

In this book, we're going to focus on how to get reviews, what to do with them, and how getting reviews are an integral part of your marketing and promotional strategy. Keep in mind, as you push through this book, some concepts are going to seem rudimentary. Hang in there because I'm laying a foundation of things to come. You must learn how to crawl before you can walk or even begin to run.

Once you finish this book, you'll have enough advice and practical steps to build more relevancy on your books with a consistent flow of reviews on the Amazon platform. I want to see you succeed beyond measure, and the best way to do that is to load you up with sensible advice. Put down your tacos, wipe off your fingers, and let's dig right into how to get more book reviews on Amazon.

*R*eviews play an integral part in the development and exposure of your book and brand. Having a review is the validation of someone experiencing your product on the Amazon marketplace. Can you still sell books without reviews? Absolutely, but you start at a greater disadvantage than other books like yours with reviews.

For instance, a customer searches for a book in their favorite genre, werebear shapeshifter romance. Amazon serves the first sixteen options on the first-page query results. In this example, one book has no reviews, while the other book has seventy-two reviews. Both covers look great. The titles seem interesting. Heck, even the book description is compelling, but the differentiating factor is the customer has one book with reviews while the other has none. Does the customer take a chance and buy a book without any social proof, or do they go with the crowd and buy the book with seventy-two reviews?

> Nothing attracts a crowd like a crowd.

People love to share the same experience with other people, especially if it's great. There's a sense of community built around an experience, whether it's a great restaurant or a good book. When people enjoy something, they want to pass that experience to other people. Conversely, when the experience is unpleasant, they're quick to urge people away from it. Each instance tells a different story and plays an integral role in other people wanting to take part.

For instance, I'm always rubbernecking in the low end of the reviews pool. Why? I get an honest look at what went wrong in the experience. When the experience is unsatisfactory, I'm curious as to why. Will my opinion vary from the reviewer, or will I agree with them?

Ultimately, reviews on Amazon play a vital role in customers making an informed purchase. Though a fraction of customers probably know what they want and skip the reviews, a large majority will skim through the reviews to see if it's a good fit. Where some authors get it wrong is the low reviews. While it sucks to hear someone trashing your book, that review reveals a bigger picture. In some cases, that low review entices a different mindset or customer to purchase it.

Here's the deal with reviews. When a customer visits your product page, they either pass, or they buy. There's no middle of the road. They have two choices and one decision to make. If the browsing customer buys, then you increase your conversion rate. What are you converting? Browsing customers into buyers. The more customers you convert, the more Amazon rewards your product page with additional traffic. The lower the conversion rate, the less traffic Amazon sends.

At the end of the day, Amazon wants to make money. If you're in it to do the same thing, then Amazon will be in your court. However, suppose you're not in it to make money or convert more customers into buyers. In that case, Amazon will move onto other authors who do align with their goal. Higher conversion rates increase your rankings in the search results, leading to more discoverability. The more discoverable your book is on Amazon, the more chances you will convert customers into buyers. It's one big vicious cycle.

How do you convert more customers into buyers? You got it – reviews! A product with five reviews is 270% more likely to sell than a product with no reviews.[16] Wow! Is that all it takes? Five reviews? Yep, even if you got your mom, her best friend, your cousin, significant other, and neighbor to leave a review. You're more likely to sell your book than your competitor, who has a big ol' fat goose egg for reviews. Of course, I'm not encouraging you to get your friends and family to leave a review. We'll address why that's not a good idea later in this book.

Other areas to consider the efficacy of having reviews is through advertising campaigns. Whether you're driving traffic natively through Amazon Advertising or delivering traffic through Facebook Ads, having your book equipped with some reviews is better than no reviews at all. There's a good reason Amazon loads up every product page with similar books and other products customers might enjoy. If your book doesn't convert a sale, Amazon still has a little more skin in the game. If you don't profit or capitalize on the traffic, then Amazon will.

Do you want to have a better return on your investment in paid advertising campaigns? Then, load your book up with reviews before you launch your next campaign. Once the traffic arrives at your book's product page, they at least have some proof other customers have read or bought your book before.

In *Amazon Keywords for Books*, I discussed the importance of relevancy. The Amazon algorithm places value on your product based on its ability to sell to customers at any given moment – also known as relevancy. The more relevant your book is, the more apt Amazon is to serve it to customers searching for it. What is the best builder in relevance for a product on Amazon? You guessed it – sales!

The more sales you get, the more relevant your title is in its given niche. What we know about relevance is that the algorithm doesn't simply rely on sales alone. Otherwise, brand new products with little to no sales would not appear in search queries. Sharing a product through social media, saving a product to wish lists, and getting reviews also play a role in building relevance.

Amazon views action taken on any given product page as a small trigger. This engagement sends a signal to the Amazon algorithm that says, "There's something about this product that other people might like."

That's where reviews come in. Every time a customer leaves a review, that sends a small signal to the Amazon algorithm. Furthermore, any keywords or commentary relative to your niche mentioned in the review also send signals to the Amazon algorithm. If someone votes for a review as helpful or comments on a review, additional signals are sent to the algorithm.

What goes up inevitably comes down. Getting reviews and engagement on a page may be effective in the moment, but it doesn't have lasting power in building relevance. That's not to say the social proof isn't as compelling on the browsing customer. Those reviews will still hold weight with the browsing customer. Similar to a balloon tossed in the air, the relevancy slowly drifts down for a product. The further out we go from a posted review, the less it affects the product's relevance.

Don't let that stop you. Should you accept it, your mission is to continue to bring in a consistent flow of reviews. That way, you prove to the Amazon algorithm how relevant your title truly is compared to other titles or books with less or older reviews. The key to building long-term sustainable relevancy in the Amazon algorithm is getting more sales. If you want more sales, then get more reviews.

Legendary guitarist, Dimebag Darrell, was once told by his father if he learned one riff a day over the year, he'd have learned 365 new riffs. Similar to Darrell, if you focus on getting one new review every day, you'll have 365 reviews in a year. If that seems impossible, then consider getting one review per week – fifty-two reviews in a year. Consistency is the name of the game. Stick to gathering reviews, and you'll have a ton of reviews to build massive social proof. Meanwhile, you'll keep the relevancy balloon afloat by tapping it up and away from the floor.

Keeping your product relevant will deliver more traffic. In turn, you should see more opportunities to sell more books. One hand washes the other, and you hopefully get more reviews.

Is it a good idea to get reviews all at once, or does it work against you? It's certainly debatable how a large influx of reviews will hurt your book. However, it does prove to Amazon the title might not have good long-term sustainability. Sure, it's great to see a title sell many books on launch day, and it's even nicer to have scores of reviews shower in after launch. What's even better is a gradual influx of reviews. Stick with it and never give up on the mission to bring in more reviews.

What about bad reviews? Do low-star reviews bring down your book? There are a couple of ways to look at this issue. If you have nothing but four and five-star reviews, browsing customers might feel suspicious. After all, we're in the day and age where fake reviews run afoul of Amazon on the regular. Having a few low reviews helps balance out a product page. Book reviews seem more authentic when there are all types of customers' experiences and mindsets shared in a review.

Where one customer might dislike a certain aspect of a book, another might find it appealing. For instance, one customer might leave a low rating and state:

> "This book was too detailed and spent way too much time describing the scene. Cut to the chase, I just want the fight scene."

Another customer might read that low review and think:

> "Well, that's just my style of reading. I hate it when writers rush into a fight scene. I like it when a writer develops the character, lays out the scene, and builds suspense to a dramatic climax."

One man's trash is another man's treasure. We often assume this phrase is only applicable to physical objects. In this instance, one person's dislike could strike the other person's fancy.

While a low review doesn't give the greatest feeling, it can serve the bigger picture. Take it with a grain of salt and remind yourself, you cannot please everyone. Once you get good with that fact, receiving the bad news of a low review becomes easier.

Good, bad, or indifferent; reviews play a large role in developing trust with your potential customer. How many you get is not as relevant as how many you get consistently over the long term. I heard a famous YouTuber state how no book will have any long-lasting power unless it had fifty reviews.

Fifty reviews, huh? This same famous YouTuber isn't prolific. She has a handful of publications. Where she gets her information is unknown. You can't discern that fifty reviews answer the long-term success when you haven't at least published hundreds of books to be statistically relevant. Ultimately, there's no hard and fast number of reviews to determine your book's long-term success. Even the previous stats I shared about five reviews versus none is somewhat anecdotal since results can vary based on the product type, the niche, and the buying audience.

Buyers like to see reviews on a product. Some reviews are better than no reviews. Never has a customer landed on a product, found the number of reviews to be below fifty, and clicked away. It's just not a thing. There's no real hard evidence the Amazon algorithm will favor a product because it has fifty reviews. What does the algorithm favor? Consistent performance. So long as the product continues to sell and get consistent reviews, the Amazon algorithm rewards that product.

Though fifty reviews are an admirable goal, once you hit the milestone, go for an even higher goal. As you're shooting for your goals, remember it will take time and consistent efforts. Along the way, you will get organic reviews. However, you shouldn't rely solely on organic reviews to keep your book relevant to Amazon.

I often hear it takes 1000 ebook downloads before you get one organic review. Wow! If that were true, it'd take you 50,000 downloads to even hit a fifty-review milestone. If you're getting 50,000 downloads or purchases, then chances are pretty likely you're getting more than organic reviews along the way. On most occasions, authors aren't even getting 50,000 downloads with a deep back catalog of books. It's sad but true.

I implore you not to be complacent. Do not rely on organic reviews and consider them more like icing on the cake. They're nice to have, but you shouldn't rely on them to happen. If you were to bank on organic reviews, your strategy needs to change from gathering reviews to selling more books. While I encourage you to pump up your book sales through marketing and promotion, you shouldn't let review gathering fall to the wayside.

I have to open this chapter with the compulsory disclaimer: Amazon didn't endorse, fund, or agree to this book. They can and will change their community guidelines. Rather than creating a brand-new edition for every change Amazon makes in their rules, I'm just going to defer you to them first. Sadly, no book will be evergreen with the ever-changing market online. Still, I'm going to do my best to give you the currently acceptable practices and recommendations according to the current Amazon Community Guidelines.

First and foremost, customers cannot post a product review without spending $50 over the past year. If you send people to leave a review, they need to spend the minimum first.[17]

A few years ago, Amazon caught wind of some bad actors posting fake reviews on product pages. It mostly involved third-party sellers and some self-publishers. These bad actors would hire outside parties to post reviews on their product page to bolster relevancy in the search engine. They tricked Amazon customers into believing their product had real reviews.

Rather than kick everyone out for posting bad reviews, Amazon placed a paywall to deter bad actors. It still hasn't entirely stopped all bad actors; it's simply slowed them down. After all, where there's a will, there's a way. Bad actors will hire outside parties plus give a $50 allowance to spend on Amazon. They can then use it to buy a ton of books, inflate the book rank, and then leave reviews wherever they want.

Here's the interesting part: anyone can leave any review on any product they wish, so long as they fulfill the $50 minimum spending threshold. That means customers don't even have to buy a specific product on Amazon to leave a review. For instance, if a customer bought your book at the local bookstore and met the Amazon minimum spending threshold, he can post a review on your book on Amazon.

However, Amazon labels the review differently based on the person's purchase history on the website. When a customer buys a product on Amazon and leaves a review, Amazon labels the review as a "Verified Purchase."

Whereas, if a customer didn't buy a product on Amazon but leaves a product review, Amazon doesn't label it. Most industry insiders refer to this type of review as an "Unverified Purchase." Anyone can leave a review on any product on Amazon. As long as a customer purchases $50 in Amazon products in the last year, he can post a review of anything.

What has more traction, the verified purchase, or unverified purchase? Amazon never states if the verified purchase tag carries any more weight than the unverified purchase review.[18] While some industry experts feel it does carry more weight in the algorithm, there's no solid proof. If we consider the customers, do they really care about the *Verified Purchase* tag? I can guarantee you most customers aren't even aware of it.

In fact, in the launch of *Amazon Keywords for Books*, quite a few readers who received an advanced reading copy weren't aware of the $50 threshold. Chances are likely they didn't even know about verified purchase reviews too. The tag isn't too conspicuous on the reviews. In some instances, it's so small on a desktop computer most people won't even notice it.

The "Verified Purchase" review tag displays a proof of purchase for the reviewer.

The day might come when Amazon has enough of the bad actors and unverified purchase reviews. Then, they will require customers to buy the product to leave a review. If a customer doesn't buy the product through Amazon, then his opinion isn't welcome. I imagine those old unverified purchase reviews would disappear, and all that would remain are the verified purchase reviews.

If you want to be on the safe side, try to get verified purchase reviews when you can. Sure, it's easier said than done, but it could very well help you out. Even if Amazon never removes the ability to post unverified purchase reviews, at least you have some verified purchase reviews for more credibility.

Biased Reviews Could Kill Your Momentum

Back when I first self-published, I naturally wanted to post a review of my product. Taking a little extra time, I crafted the perfect review of my first book. Once I posted the review, I was sure it'd create more intrigue and draw prospective buyers. I waited a day or two to see if it'd post on my book's product page, and nothing surfaced.

Realizing it might seem kind of sad to review my own book, I reached out to my wife to post a review. She, too, wrote up a brilliant review and posted it. This time the review stuck, but within a few days, the review disappeared. Undeterred, she tried again with the same results.

Naturally, I contacted Amazon support only to find out one glaring issue. If Amazon detects a direct relationship between a product and a buyer, they determine the review as biased. While posting a review of my own book is rather sad, it's also very biased. Amazon does not want biased reviews. The relationship between a seller and a customer influences the review. Amazon doesn't want any of that bias. After all, the customer isn't going to remain impartial.

Your mother, brother, sister, wife, close friends, or anyone who's currently living with you will stand to gain something out of leaving a positive review. That just won't work. Amazon simply wants candid thoughts from customers who don't stand to gain anything out of leaving a review. As a customer, I'm sure you would agree too. You don't want to buy a product when all you see are positive marks posted by the seller's mother. Any customer wants real insights and reflections so he can make an informed purchase without coercion or shenanigans.

What constitutes a biased review beyond people you directly know? Well, the guidelines get a bit gray, and the automated systems indicate a double standard. Amazon has what appears to be an automated system vetting reviews posted on its platform. If a seller and buyer share the same Amazon account, physical address, bank account, or credit card, Amazon deems the review biased. Instantly, the review is null and void.

Amazon also flags reviews as biased for what the reviewer states. If a reviewer posts a specific word or phrase indicating a direct relationship, they'll pull it. The company isn't fully disclosing what those words or phrases are. It makes sense for Amazon to keep those words and phrases undisclosed, so bad actors don't have the opportunity to work their way around the system.

We could assume any word or phrase indicating a direct relationship would be off the table. If a reviewer states he's your best friend and loves your book, don't be surprised when Amazon pulls the review down. If you have a reader who posted a review, it's going to be up to that reader to address the removed review, not you. It only further complicates the situation and proves a direct relationship when you get involved.

Ultimately, we're subject to the whim of a machine that detects bias, and we have no control over what it deems as biased or not. Rather than sweat the system, keep pushing forward and gathering reviews that will stick. You can always direct your reader to address the issue with Amazon at community-help@amazon.com.

Friends & Family Are Killing Your Book

New authors should bask in the admiration of their peers, friends, and family when they first publish a book. It's quite the feat and not something too many people can or will do. I won't take anything away from the power of having a great support network. When you publish your first book, everyone and your mother will want a copy for prosperity's sake.

Sadly, your friends and family are killing the relevancy of your book. We already know getting a review from your family is a no-go. If Amazon detects a direct relationship, the review will never see the light of day.

For the sake of argument, let's say your friends and family have no issue leaving a review, and the review sticks with no further complication. That's all well and good, except now, you confused the Amazon algorithm. Previously covered in *Amazon Keywords for Books*, the algorithm is a machine-generated formula tracking buyer behaviors and predicting outcomes on the platform. The algorithm is largely responsible for predicting and serving up products customers will most likely want to buy.

No, you didn't confuse the Amazon algorithm with undetected, yet biased reviews. You confused the algorithm when you allowed your friends and family to buy your book. Though your friends and family love you and have your back, they may not necessarily enjoy the type of content you write. Rarely do your writing interests overlap with your family or friends' reading interests. Therein lies the problem.

When you have a friend or family member support you when buying and reviewing your book, you're having them confuse the algorithm. Where the Amazon algorithm expects specific buy patterns based on your family and friends' buy history, a curveball comes out of nowhere.

For example, suppose your mother normally buys books based on gardening and products for her garden. In that case, the Amazon algorithm serves products to her based on her interests in gardening. Once your mom buys your book based on adult baby diaper lover (ABDL) romance, she confuses the algorithm. The Amazon machine needs to figure out the sudden shift in buying and reviewing patterns, and then it tries to match up your ABDL romance book with other gardeners. You can imagine most gardeners will give that ABDL romance book a hard pass, thereby decreasing relevancy in the search engine.

Avoid selling your books to friends and family and having them leave a review. If they must buy your book, then let them do it. I wouldn't recommend pushing them to leave a review. Just leave it alone and go on without it.

The Bias in Social Media

Now more than ever, building an author platform requires having a presence on social media. As an author, you can create a stronger bond with your readers, develop a sense of community, and grow your author brand quicker than ever.

Lurking in Facebook Groups, online forums, and chats is a bit of an enigma – bias through social media. Some authors believe Amazon tracks all online social media activity. The theory is if an author and reader connect in any way via social media, Amazon strikes down any review posted.

This theory means if you and your reader are friends on Facebook, then Amazon deems this a direct relationship. Therefore, any review posted by your reader has a bias. In 2015, a reader had some issues with review removal. This reader followed her favorite author on social media. That was the only direct connection she could draw to why the review disappeared.[19]

Some people even speculate if a reader likes an author's business page, Amazon views it as a direct relationship. It's no surprise how it's harder than ever to separate fact from fiction. Meanwhile, Amazon isn't being entirely transparent about its methods for determining bias in reviews. When pressed for an answer, Amazon simply states a detection of a direct relationship.

How is Amazon able to police such a large area, and is it legal? These are certainly questions worth considering for another book altogether. For now, let's focus on what we can do to mitigate any issues. It all starts with the direct correlation between Amazon and social media.

For starters, Amazon bought the social media platform for readers called Goodreads in 2013. One of the ways users can log into Goodreads is through a Facebook login. This integration opens up more questions about how Amazon and Facebook could be data mining together in a collaborative effort. During this data mining, can Amazon see who associates with whom on the Facebook platform?

Dave Chesson, of the YouTube channel Kindlepreneur,[20] even questioned this potential correlation between Goodreads and Facebook. When a review disappears, and the only trackable evidence comes down to this relationship between social media platforms, it makes you wonder. When setting up a Goodreads account, Dave recommends you avoid signing in with Facebook, and use an altogether different login.

This safeguard is something you can always share with your readers. Still, it's certainly not something you should make part of your review gathering methods. I simply want to shed light on potential reasons reviews might disappear from your book's product page.

Review Swaps Are the Worst

In the early days of publishing on Amazon, authors could get more reviews through a quid pro quo system called review swapping. One author could exchange books with another author. They'd each read the book and then leave an honest review on the product page. Both authors walked away happy, and life was good.

Sadly, what was once a good idea, turned into a bad idea quickly. Bad actors rolled in and bastardized the system. Rather than exchanging with other authors, the bad actors hired outside workers to do their dirty work. Instead of reading the book, the hired help (aka virtual assistants) reached out to other authors or people in their field. They do the exchange and post a review despite never having read the book.

In some instances, the book reviews often appear stilted and are pretty bland like, "This is a good book. I would recommend it to you. You should buy this book. You would like it too."

Author review swaps are in direct violation of the Amazon Community Guidelines. You must not coerce or pay for reviews. If you do either of those, you stand to lose a lot. In fact, I know first-hand the consequences.

In 2014, everyone and their mother published books on the Kindle Direct Publishing (KDP) platform. Anyone could publish just about any level of hammered garbage and profit hand over fist. Naturally, overnight success stories and would-be experts cropped up, seemingly popping out of the woodwork. The name of the game was to make as much money as you could regardless of the rules Amazon laid out. Part of the bad advice was to get reviews through author review swaps.

Naively, I bought in despite knowing author review swaps were, at the very least, garnering biased reviews for my titles. Having to connect with authors and getting to know them personally would imply I had a direct relationship. Yet, I soldiered forward confident I wasn't hurting anyone. The more reviews I racked up for my title, the more my books sold and climbed the charts. It seemed like the fun would never end until it did.

Around June 2015, word spread about Amazon clamping down on fake reviews and author review swaps. By this time, I was running on all cylinders. I easily read dozens of books and painstakingly crafted beautiful reviews for the authors. I even scaled it up to a point where I hired a virtual assistant to alleviate the workload. Hiring out would be my undoing.

One day, I checked into one of my books to verify a posted review from an author swap. Not only was the review gone, but scores of reviews vanished. Primarily, the bad and poorly written reviews were the ones to disappear. My heart sank, and a feeling of defeat set in.

"That's okay," I thought, "at least I still have my reviews."

Fat chance! I opened my Amazon Reviewer profile to discover all my reviews weren't there. Every last review I posted since using Amazon – from books to supplements to movies – was history. I knew I was in trouble. After repeated attempts to contact Amazon over a few days, I finally received a response.

Amazon called me out for manipulating the reviews system and permanently banned me from using any of the Amazon Community features. As you can imagine, I lost reviewing privileges, commenting privileges, and the ability to partake in any future programs of the Amazon Community.

All this had to do was over my impatience to get reviews the legitimate way. Folks do not, under any circumstances, pay for an Amazon review or post a fake review. They will catch you, and they will enforce their community guidelines. To this day, I nervously look over my shoulder, wondering if this misdeed will create an issue with my other Amazon accounts. Could it affect all my Amazon accounts, including KDP, Merch by Amazon, Amazon Associates, Prime Video Direct, Media on Demand, and Twitch? Only time will tell.

If you're going to get reviews, do it without an exchange of money or through coercive practices like review swapping. It'll land you in hot water. Though my story seems pretty serious, it pales in comparison to the controversy surrounding a famous indie author, Chance Carter.

Bribes for Reviews

Around mid-2018, Amazon rolled out changes based on incentivizing reviews. What were the grounds for this sudden change? Authors were actively soliciting their readers for reviews. On the surface, asking your readers for reviews seems okay. That is until you bribe them. Romance author Chance Carter openly solicited his readers with the prospect of winning *Tiffany's Jewelry*. With proof of a posted review, Carter entered his readers in a giveaway for free jewelry. Enticing readers with the prospect of winning jewelry clearly creates biased reviews. In turn, the reviews will come out in favor of the book and the author.[21]

When Amazon caught wind of this indiscretion, they closed up the loophole. Chance Carter faced updating a deep backlist of titles. The lesson is, don't try to bribe or coerce your readers into leaving a review. You will get burned and have fewer reviews than when you started. Besides, do you really want to blow your marketing budget on jewelry for your readers? I think that's a bit overboard for reviews alone.

Without incentivizing or having any direct relationship with the reader, how can you get book reviews then? Surely, it can't be as hard as some people make it out to be, is it? Let's dive into the best first steps in getting reviews – inside the book.

When getting reviews, start with the path of least resistance. Meet your readers precisely where they're at – inside the book. Where you place it and how you ask are the most important aspects of getting reviews. Just remember, you don't want to deviate too far off the beaten path or go south of Amazon's Community Guidelines.

The best way to get reviews is simply to ask. That's it! Nothing fancy. The answer is always "no" if you never ask, and this area is no exception to the rule. Your approach is going to make the most difference. Simply asking alone won't get many results. Then again, if you go too long in your ask, you might get a lot of readers tuning out, especially where I'm going to have you insert it.

All ebooks on Amazon finish with a call-to-action (CTA) by Amazon to post a review. Even if you didn't follow my instructions, you could feel confident you have safety measures in place. Also, Amazon has readers sign into their associated Goodreads accounts. Then, readers can post on Amazon and Goodreads.

However, the reality is most readers won't finish your book. For that matter, some readers will most likely finish the last chapter and whatever comes after is inessential. The back matter of the book is what readers often overlook. The inessential content to them includes the author's bio, the special thanks, the resources, and the additional promotion of your other books.

If a reader is most likely to tune out after flipping the final page, we need to strike while the iron is hot! As soon as your book finishes, you need to lead with a CTA. Ask them for the review immediately after the last chapter. You only have one opportunity, so make the most of it.

Lead with a bold headline that commands their attention. Think about making the headline no more than five to six words long. If you're good at copywriting, then now is your time to shine! If you're like me and don't have the skillset, that's okay. Try your best.

The next thing is to keep it short. I recently checked out an indie author's book and discovered their CTA for leaving a review was over a page and a half long. No! I'm not reading your CTA. After all, I just finished your book, so what makes you think I'm going to read something that has no real intrinsic value for me? You need to lead with the goods.

Keep it simple. For instance:

> Now that you finished reading this book, it'd be a huge favor to me, and future readers, if you left feedback on Amazon.
>
> While I have no expectations on what kind of review you leave, it'd certainly make my day knowing you read the whole book and shared your honest experience with the world.
>
> You can post a review on Amazon or at Amazon.com/gp/product-review/B08HMCNKVT.

Feel free to swipe the copy above if you want, but I recommend rewording and rewriting it in a way to make sense for your book and brand.

Again, I'm not a copywriter, so you may want to consider dressing yours up in a more enticing way. The keys to a good CTA for reviewing include:

- Bold headline

- Brevity

- Outbound link

The last key to getting the review is to remove any hurdles for your reader. Instead of having your reader search for where to leave a review, send them right to the source. Sure, you could tell them to flip all the way to the back until Amazon asks them to leave a review. Might I suggest having them do less, though? Simply use an outbound link, and it's quite simple. The formula for the review website URL is:

Amazon.com/gp/product-review/(Insert your book ASIN here)

Let's first address the ASIN or American Standard Identification Number. The ASIN is the code associated with your book once you publish it to the Amazon platform. You can access it in your Kindle Direct Publishing dashboard next to your book or on your book's product page in the "Product Details" section. You will not have the ASIN until you publish the book.

Here's where I'm going to save you a lot of time and heartache. In *Promotional Strategies for Books*, I shared the importance of getting your own website and custom domain name. Furthermore, I suggested installing Pretty Links, a WordPress plug-in, so you could create subdirectories (i.e., dalelinks.com/checklist). Now, we're going to put your domain name to work.

Instead of having to update your publications when they launch with an unmemorable hyperlink, you're going to use a custom URL to redirect readers to the review page. For example, in *Amazon Keywords for Books*, my CTA for reviews included the link DaleLinks. com/ReviewKeywordsBook. Though the link wasn't working when I uploaded the ebook and print book, I had it working as soon as I knew the ASIN of my book.

You'll take the long Amazon link, add your ASIN to the end, and use your custom domain to redirect to the review page. You're done! This link will work for reviewing both your ebook and print book. If you don't fix the link right away, it's not a big deal. You won't have to sweat anyone using the review link right away since it's at the end of the book. And, no one will skip to the end once they buy it in the first twenty-four hours anyway.

Just make sure you don't forget to create the custom domain redirect as soon as your book is live on Amazon. That way, you aren't panicking later when you realize the custom domain isn't set.

The nice thing is you'll have a web address you can recommend your readers visit. Share it in your email newsletter, on social media, or in a video interview. The options are limitless.

The smartest thing to do is use a custom domain name with brand recognition and make the subdirectory easily memorable. Don't put a ton of initials, numbers, or acronyms. You want people to remember it or trust it when they see it.

While posting a CTA in the back of your book might seem rather innocuous, it's much better than trying to go without it. Also, I find it mind-blowing how authors don't have this simple feature in their books. Inserting a CTA in a book seems like a given to most indie authors. Yet, quite a few authors who struggle to get reviews aren't even doing it. Don't be that guy. Insert a CTA in the back of your book. You'll thank me later.

*N*ow that you have a fundamental understanding of reviews, and how to get them, it's time to break outside your inner circle and reach out into the world. Where do you look, who can you trust, and what should you say?

The first place to look is through a simple Google search. Type in your niche and book reviews. Skip the ads. We're only interested in a specific type of book reviewer. Some readers loyally follow and support their favorite niche. On their websites or blogs, they share candid reviews of what they've read. On many occasions, they don't cost a dime, and quite frankly, they shouldn't. Remember, we don't want to pay for reviews posted on Amazon.

Next, dig through the blogger's website to verify the type of reviews they do. Some of them only post reviews to their websites while others post on Amazon as well. It's not a deal-breaker for me if they don't post to Amazon. I'm less apt to send the first review copies to readers who aren't actively posting on Amazon. I may come back to them later once I have courted all the active Amazon reviewers.

Do a little research ahead, and it will pay off in the long run. If a blogger has an Amazon reviewer profile, read through their old reviews. You're looking for a historical pattern. Some reviewers are fairly balanced and will leave a mix of good and bad reviews. Then, other reviewers might leave a ton of low reviews or nothing but high reviews. I tend to avoid anyone with a profile with historically low reviews. This reader tends to be fickle and not worth approaching. If you see an average of four to five-star reviews, then this reader might be a good fit!

Now, search for any contact information and guidelines. You can find most of this info on the main landing page or the about page of the website. It might take a minute or two but can be worth it. Once you have the info you need, reach out to them. I'll explain how you pitch it once you consider other avenues to contact reviewers.

We're in a new age where video is king online! If you can land a review with a video creator, you've greatly increased your odds of getting more sales. YouTube, Facebook Live, Twitch, Periscope, and any other video platform are places to start. You'll search just as you did on Google. This time pay the closest attention to video creators with a history of posting book reviews.

YouTube has a growing community of video creators aptly named BookTubers (or BookTube). Their main focus is on books. They read books, share books they buy, and interact with other readers. Think of it as a Book Club, but on video. Again, focus on BookTubers actively posting reviews on Amazon and are familiar with your niche. You don't want to send a review copy of your werebear shapeshifter romance book if the BookTuber primarily talks about science fiction fantasy books.

The next best people to contact are podcasters. Downloadable audio has been an upward trend, and it seems almost everyone has a podcast about something these days. Do the same simple Google search you did for book review sites, but this time look for podcasts instead of book reviewers. If you happen to find a podcaster who does reviews, then great! In most instances, you just want to find a podcast relevant to your niche. Then, it's up to you to do the outreach.

Asking for a Review from a Complete Stranger

Do you remember the call-to-action we placed in the back of your book? We're going to use the same methodology in asking for a review. You won't need a special link. In fact, you won't even need to send any content when you're cold prospecting.

The key to outreach is brevity. You must respect the potential readers' time. Imagine how easy it is to find them. Now think about how many other authors are contacting them for reviews. Respect their time, and it may pay off in dividends.

When it comes to what you say, I recommend you speak from the heart. You don't need to go into too much detail. If you've done your research, you can probably lead with how you found the reviewer and what you like best about their content. The next step is to skip right to the chase. Why are you contacting them, and what's in it for them?

Don't beat around the bush. You're looking for readers who'd be willing to read a complimentary copy in hopes of getting honest reviews posted on Amazon. That's it! Don't worry about Jedi mind tricks or writing the best ad copy to entice them to accept your offer.

Here's an example:

Hey, Dale,

Your YouTube channel popped up while I was kicking around online, and I noticed you're a big fan of werebear shapeshifter romance.

I'd love to get your feedback on my upcoming release called "Werebear versus Werewolf."

If you're game, I could send you a copy right away.

Thanks for your time, and I'm looking forward to hearing back from you.

Did you notice how brief I kept it? It didn't take much time to type it. Simultaneously, the recipient won't feel overwhelmed by an epic-length email that doesn't get to the point. Cut to the chase, and you'll waste less of everyone's time.

Do not send a copy to your prospect without getting permission. I know it seems easy to attach your ebook to an email. Still, nothing seems fishier than an email from a random stranger with an attachment. Whenever I get an email with an attachment from a stranger, I toss it into my spam folder.

Also, some reviewers have a format preference. You'll want to have your ebook available in PDF, epub, and mobi, so it's readable across all devices. I typically upload all three formats into a zipped file with instructions on downloading the preferred file to mobile. Then, I put the zipped file into a cloud drive and generate a shareable link for the potential reviewer.

Another reason to avoid sending out a manuscript without permission is some reviewers prefer hard copies of your book. Quite frankly, a vast majority of readers still prefer print books. The part you need to consider is, can you afford to send out print copies? You'll have to account for all the costs. Sending out a review copy through Amazon is one way and probably the cheapest solution if you have Amazon Prime. Another way is to order bulk copies and then send out the review copy. The latter method requires a bit more money and hassle.

The issue with gifting a copy to a reviewer from your own account is that Amazon might deem the review biased. Because of the connection between you and the reader through your Amazon purchase, Amazon can then assume you know this person directly. Sadly, the more costly and difficult option of ordering copies in advance might be the better option for review longevity.

It's not to say you can't gift print copies or ebooks to a reviewer. I've done it many times with no issue with the reviews sticking. Consider two factors in the efficacy of that review:

- The reader will post a review from their account, so the review will be an unverified purchase

- If the reader has the same address on file for their Amazon account as the one you shipped to, Amazon might deem it as biased

There's no real way of telling how Amazon enforces it. If you want to err on the side of caution, simply fulfill the print shipment yourself.

Some time ago, I gathered reviews for my book *An Ultimate Home Workout Plan Bundle*. For whatever reason, I felt sending print copies to every reviewer was a great idea. I reached out to several reviewers on Amazon, a few bloggers, and various influencers. All in all, I invested over $300 in about thirty-six review copies. These three mistakes were the result:

1. Investing in print copies when I couldn't even afford the expense.

2. Neglecting the ebook option.

3. I didn't account for the review copy ratio. You'll learn more about that next.

Gathering Reviews: The Numbers Game

In most instances, getting reviews is a numbers game. The more people you ask, the better. I found one out of every three readers will post a review after receiving a complimentary copy. This includes following up with readers. Some readers will be on top of posting their reviews. Most readers will spend their time doing other things outside of reading the book. A fraction of readers will simply become unresponsive. Yes, it's the harsh truth, you can send out free stuff to someone, and they'll stop talking to you.

Indie author Alinka Rutkowska shared in a post on Kindlepreneur.com about her experience in getting reviews. She discussed how getting reviews is a numbers game. Only one in three readers will post a review even when the agreement was to post a review for getting a complimentary copy. If you want 300 reviews, then you're going to need to get 900 readers for your book. [22]

Do not make the same mistakes I did. Never invest money into review gathering you can't stand to lose. Offer the ebook before suggesting the print book is available. Sending out ebooks is way more cost-effective and less time-consuming than print books. Lastly, never expect to get all readers to post a review. I never heard of any author having a 100% return on their review efforts. If a reader doesn't post a review, put them on a *Do Not Contact* list and move on.

When you find a reviewer who posts a review and doesn't need prompting, hang onto them. Cherish that reader and show your appreciation. No, you don't have to shower them with jewelry. A simple thanks via email will suffice, or even classier, a short video. If the person is an influencer, YouTuber, or blogger, it behooves you to showcase their review and promote their brand. That's the best gratitude you can give to influencers.

The Follow-Up Sequence

One area to further consider is your follow-up sequence. You need to build reasonable time to follow up after the reader receives your review copy. Ask the reader when a good time is to follow up with them. Don't

Overthink it. The reader is attending to other things outside of reading your book. If you have a standard-length book between 20,000 and 40,000 words, then a month should be sufficient. A reader will need considerably more time with an epic-length novel. The best way to know how long it'll take a reader is to ask them. That's it!

When I follow up, I do it once and move on. I won't bother with hounding readers about leaving reviews. I'd rather spend time writing my next book, gathering more reviews, or promoting my other books. Trying to micromanage readers is time-consuming and, quite frankly, comes off as desperate. It's not a good look, so follow up once, then move on.

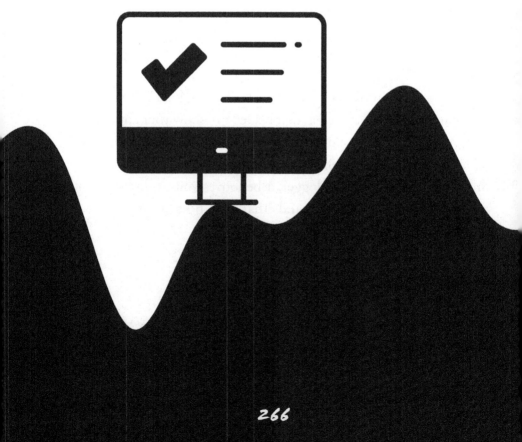

*C*hasing after influencers, bloggers, and YouTubers can be tiring. Part of why it sucks comes from the act of cold prospecting. If you're anything like me, then you most likely despise being salesy or coming off as pushy. That predisposition tends to make most people avoid cold prospecting altogether. It's not that cold prospecting is bad. It's just hard work. You'll get more no's than yes's. Even when they accept you, you'll face the harsh reality that only one in three readers leaves a review.

That's okay because I have your solution - an advanced reader copy team! Also known as an ARC team, the advanced reader copy team is an elite group of readers who receive your manuscript before the public. The ARC team functions in two ways:

- Early feedback

- Immediate reviews after publishing

Getting early feedback from readers can help you fine-tune any small discrepancies. For instance, when I launched *Amazon Keywords for Books,* I reached out to about twelve followers. I had these twelve readers opt into the ARC team by way of StoryOrigin. They had the option to download any ebook format – epub, mobi, or PDF. Within the first twenty-four hours, I found a litany of issues with the manuscript. Between formatting errors, missing text, and typos, I snuffed out those issues well before it hit the buying public.

I guess you could say your ARC team functions as a last line of defense in proofreading before the book goes public. Be mindful of what your ARC readers say and the problems they point out. Don't get defensive. After all, they're helping you free of charge. If you don't understand the criticism, have the reader clarify. It's better to know than to assume.

The second most important function of an ARC team is getting reviews out on launch day. These reviews are critical in lending credibility as soon as your book goes live on the Amazon Marketplace. Once browsing customers land on your product page, they'll see immediately other people read your book. That warm, fuzzy feeling of knowing another reader consumed your book is more validation working in your favor.

How exactly do you build an ARC team? What if you don't have a following? Is this even possible for all authors? It requires a deeper explanation. In short, ARC teams should be part of any author's book launch strategy. Without one, you're taking a gamble and hoping Amazon will push your book based on keyword and niche selection alone.

Building an Email List

Email marketing is a vehicle all authors need to have in their marketing and promotion toolbox. By using services like Mailchimp, MailerLite, ConvertKit, and the like, you can solicit your readers to subscribe to your email newsletter. In *Promotional Strategies for Books*, I shared insights on the best ways to build and grow an email list.

In brief, email marketing is a safeguard for your business. Though people who read your books are your readers, they are not your customers.

They are Amazon's customers. It's the cold, hard truth. If Amazon should ever deem you unfit to be on their platform, they can and will kick you off the platform without any recourse. Rather than tempt fate, you should put a system in place that converts your readers into your followers. How do you do that? Email marketing!

Now it doesn't require a ton of coding or technical know-how. All you need to do is join any number of email marketing services available. Then, create a simple opt-in page through the platform. Once you complete the landing page, your email marketing platform will give you a URL or web address. Share that link with your readers.

Start with inserting a call-to-action (CTA) in the front and back of your book. Place a short prompt before your introduction. Having it in your book's front matter helps, especially since most people will not read an entire book. For my front matter CTA, I lead with something compelling and an offer the reader can't refuse. Try to entice them with a special offer for subscribing to your email newsletter. It could be something as simple as:

> Want to know the secret to publish less while profiting more?
>
> Then download a free copy to the Smart Publisher's Black Book when you subscribe to Dale's VIP Reader's Club.
>
> Visit DaleLinks.com/Checklist to join today!

Though it's a crude example, an offer like this one works, nonetheless. The main thing is to attract the type of email subscribers you want, so only offer what you can deliver and what interests them most. If you're dry on ideas on how to entice your readers, then try something like:

Do you want to get updated news about publishing, discounts, and advanced copies?

Then, join Dale's VIP Reader's Club at DaleLinks.com/SignUp.

Some email marketing experts would lose their minds over this simple CTA because you'll get fewer email subscribers. Don't worry about what they think. The best part of a simple CTA is you're going to get the cream of the crop--the super-fans. These are folks who don't need much reason to join your email newsletter. On most occasions, building a list on a simple CTA will be a more engaged list.

The primary goal of building an email list is so you can take your readers with you wherever you wish to go. It's your insurance policy against the worst. The next goal is to engage, interact, and deliver value with your email subscribers. It's not enough to get them to subscribe to your email newsletter. You must interact with them. How do you measure the effectiveness of your email marketing efforts? You need to get your subscribers opening the emails, clicking on your offers, and possibly buying what you have to offer.

Building an ARC Team with Your Email List

The best first step in building an ARC team with your email list is by asking for advanced readers in an email campaign. You don't need to do anything fancy. Just ask if anyone would be interested in getting advanced copies of your book. Don't sweat having to explain how it works. You don't need to muddy up the waters with the intricacies. Just get interested readers.

You can handle interested parties in one of two ways:

1. Have your subscribers reply to your email and segment their email from the main email list. Every email marketing platform has different ways to segment an email list, so visit their FAQ section to find out how to do it.

2. You can send them to an ARC management platform. We'll discuss those options in a bit.

Long before there were ARC management platforms, I relied on segmenting my email subscribers who wanted to participate in the ARC team. To make sure I kept them in the loop on special deals, I usually moved them to a separate list altogether.

Let's say you don't want to fuss with the tire kickers and freebie seekers. Then, you may want to segment your email audience right away. You can start by segmenting your audience down to subscribers who have opened your email the most in the past thirty to ninety days. That means they're at least interested in reading your content. If you want to identify the subscribers most invested in your content, then identify subscribers who click on the most outbound links. These subscribers have proven they want to read your email and trust you enough to click on a recommended outbound link.

With segmentation comes the harsh reality you won't reach as many subscribers, but you'll remove the less motivated subscribers and skip right to the most interested ones. Think of it as a way of rewarding your subscribers for being extra cool in supporting you.

Once you have your hyper-engaged subscribers, send out your offer to join the ARC team. Keep the offer simple and straight to the point. It's not enough for you to ask them to join. You'll need to tell them what they get. Share what the book is, the potential release date, and maybe a short blurb about it. Have them reply to your email or click on a specific link to send them to a sign-up page.

Once a subscriber opts in to your ARC team, set expectations. Explain to them how an advanced reader copy works. You have to clearly state you're giving an advanced copy, hoping they'll leave a review. Don't tell them you require positive reviews or that they post on an exact date. Amazon gets a little finicky when you coerce readers into leaving reviews. If you find a reader isn't posting a review as you want, simply remove them from the ARC team.

At some point, you want to track the reviews. I use a simple spread-sheet through Google Sheets to track each ARC team member's name and email address. Ask your ARC team member what their Amazon reviewer name is. Once they post a review, you can then track it without having them report back. The less the ARC team has to do beyond reading and posting a review, the better. Though I still suggest asking the reader report back to you once they left a review. It isn't a requirement, but it certainly makes life easy in tracking each review.

Follow up with your ARC team once before your book launches to let them know about the impending launch. Then, notify your ARC team after you publish your book. Let them know it's time to post their reviews. Again, don't push them to leave any type of review. Just encourage them to leave a review and share their thoughts, whether positive or negative.

After your book launches and your team posts reviews, keep an eye on who follows through. Give your ARC team at least a week to post the reviews. After the week is up, you can send a final follow-up and showcase some of the best reviews so far. That will get anyone lagging to finally post a review. Once you've sent out the last follow-up, remove any non-performing ARC team members. You don't need to send a break-up email, and don't worry about telling them they're gone. They'll simply know you removed them when they see future books posted without getting early access.

Building an ARC Team Through Website Services

Years ago, the option for building an ARC team beyond your email list wasn't as accessible. Using a website devoted to building an ARC team is a no-brainer. You don't have to worry about micromanaging your ARC team. The website handles all the review tracking and emails. You can continue to do other things outside of ARC team management.

Between BookSprout, BookFunnel, Prolific Works, and one I'm actively using, StoryOrigin, you have plenty of options. The biggest issue is going to come down to what you need and what discretionary expense you have. Remember, your time is finite, so do you want to painstakingly track an ARC team or have someone else do it for you.

The last major publication and hard launch I did was in 2016. I was happy to find options when jumping back into the game to release *Amazon Keywords for Books*. I didn't have to rely entirely on my email list. Even though I had an email list, I didn't want the hassle of hosting the ebook files, distributing it, tracking reviews, and the rest.

Naturally, I reached out to my friend Evan Gow at StoryOrigin. At the time of this book, StoryOrigin remains in open beta with free access to all the features. Since I was new to the service, it required a little trial and error.

To find the best services for your needs, you need to consider these options:

- **File storage** — Will the platform host your ebook files? What are the file size limitations?

- **Email acquisition** — Will the platform collect ARC readers' emails, and can you get access to those emails?

- **Follow up** — Will the platform follow up with your ARC team when your book launches?

- **Review tracking** — Does the platform track reviews? What types of reviews does the platform track beyond Amazon?

I discovered a few problems right away when using StoryOrigin. For *Amazon Keywords for Books*, I had a rather large file size due to the high-resolution images. I had to get with my interior formatting team to create a compressed version of the files. In turn, I needed to disclose a slight deviation in the files with future ARC team members. I didn't want potential team members to think they were getting the full file size that the buying public would get.

StoryOrigin was largely responsible for helping launch my first book, getting over 50 reviews in the first 60 days.

The next issue I ran into was I didn't get the emails from each sub-scriber. Once the ARC team member posted a review, then I had access to them. At first, I was a bit sad, but when I reflected on it, I'd rather keep ARC members who have posted a review versus those who haven't. Sadly, I'll have to earmark the ARC members who didn't leave a review, so I reject them on future projects.

The final issue I have is the ARC team I built was only good for the current project. I couldn't simply carry the current ARC team over to the next project. Evan simply said I could reach out to those who left a review on the first project to join the new ARC team on the second project.

One of the nice parts about managing your ARC team yourself without a website service is moving the ARC team from one book project to the next without much fall off. This isn't a deal-breaker and will separate the wheat from the chaff. That's why I chose to stay with StoryOrigin. Oh, and it's free right now. I mean, come on! It's free! Can you blame me?

As for the other services, I hear a lot of good things about BookSprout. They run their services based on a tier system. You can get up to fifty reviews for about $10 per month. That's nice if you want to figure out the cost based on the review ratio shared earlier. If one in every three readers leave a review, then you can build an ARC team of up to 150 members and pay about $10 per month. Should you get more than fifty reviews, you pay $20 per month and the privilege of unlimited reviews.

If you're brand new to self-publishing and review gathering, I rec-ommend sticking to what you can afford. While it's nice to have all the extra features in a premium service, you need to be realistic with where you are as an author. If free options are all you can afford, look into StoryOrigin or other no-cost alternatives.

*A*re paid reviews okay for your book on Amazon? According to Amazon Community Guidelines, you should not pay for any reviews posted on Amazon. While this rule is abundantly clear, many websites and services confuse authors with their contradictory information.

Why aren't paid reviews okay with Amazon? The online marketplace believes receiving payment in exchange for a review opens the door to many bad actors. If it's as simple as paying for a review, couldn't the person with the most money rise to the top of the charts?

Amazon wants a level playing field for all authors and sellers on their marketplace. Getting paid reviews is a no-go because many people would abuse this power and post fake reviews. However, some sites will have you believe otherwise. Let's address each type of paid service and sift through the good and the bad.

Paid Review Sites & Services

These types of services are cut and dry. You'll typically know who runs a good or bad service based on their claims. If a website promises a certain amount of reviews, then it's probably not a legitimate service. As you already learned, getting reviews is a numbers game. Though we can expect one out of every three readers to leave a review, it's not always guaranteed. Humans are imperfect, life gets in the way, and some readers will fall through.

When a website or service promises to deliver a set number of reviews, they have something happening behind the scenes. I spoke with one such service provider. His services offered guaranteed reviews and even had a guaranteed bestsellers service package. When asked how he could guarantee a set number of reviews, he shared that in-house staff would cover any missing reviews. Essentially, it came down to paying for a review if you aren't soliciting to a group of readers.

When you pay a reader to read your book, there will be a certain level of bias. There is an exception to paid reviews we'll discuss. For now, any time a service provider promises an exact number of readers and reviews, I'm always leery and cautious about using them.

Never, under any circumstances, hire a freelancer to review your book. Again, this comes down to a clear violation of Amazon guidelines. At least with the former option, you have some separation between you, the service provider, and the potential readers. With freelance websites, you actively violate the Amazon Guidelines. Should you get caught, you'll face the same consequences I did.

Then you have virtual assistant services that specialize in getting reviews. This area gets a bit dicey, and if you aren't careful, you could be in violation. It's okay to hire a virtual assistant to find readers to review books. You must consider how they are getting those reviews. Are they active in Facebook Groups, online forums, or book clubs? Then, you might be okay.

If the virtual assistant is simply exchanging books with other virtual assistants, then that's in clear violation of the policy. You're paying a person to act on your behalf to get fake reviews. It's a no-win situation.

I encourage you to hire a virtual assistant to help manage your self-publishing business if you can afford it. Before you have your assistant gather reviews, make sure you set expectations. Discuss quality control measures to keep good reviews coming in from real readers. You do not want other virtual assistants to post reviews. A sensible way to use a virtual assistant is for community outreach, such as the methods previously mentioned in this book.

Author & Reader Websites

The next type of sites and services are for authors and readers. I encourage you to explore options where websites build a haven for readers to connect with an author. Of course, you have the ARC websites mentioned earlier, but they don't necessarily have a built-in organic reading audience. Those sites merely act as a go-between for authors to get their books to readers. It's entirely up to the author to deliver the traffic.

Author/reader websites will have a clear entry point for authors and readers like Reedsy Discovery. Another example would be a new startup called Pubby.co. Developed and founded by a former CreateSpace employee, Pubby acts as a bridge between author and readers through a unique rewards program. The more a reader participates, the more reward points they receive. Those same rewards points are good for unique opportunities for authors and their readers.

Finding a reputable author and reader website can be tough and require some research. When you're stuck, you can always refer to the Alliance of Independent Authors (ALLi). This company is a non-profit organization based in the UK run by indie authors for indie authors. They spend time researching and curating a list of service providers and websites through their Watchdog Program. When in doubt, cross-check a website or service through their Watchdog Services Directory (DaleLinks.com/Watchdog).

In fact, you can use their free service to investigate all services mentioned in this book. When I can't find a service or website on the list, I'll either pass or request an examination of the services. It's free to submit to ALLi and greatly helps other indie authors make informed decisions.

Editorial Reviews

Suppose you're looking for more premium level reviews from credible sources and authorities in publishing. In that case, editorial reviews are for you. To be clear, you will not get an editorial review posted on Amazon. Editorial reviews are only good for exposure and feedback away from Amazon.

In most editorial review services, you'll get the most detailed analysis of your book. These services focus on your niche, your writing style, any packaging, and even on some book descriptions.

Do not order an editorial review if you don't want to be hyper-analyzed. Since editorial review services commonly work with traditional publishing companies, their readers tend to be more discerning and critical. Where you might have the best editor and proofreader known to man, an editorial reviewer will spot even the slightest transgression in your work.

Since editorial reviews don't appear on Amazon, what function does it serve? Most services have additional perks to showcase the book on their website, email newsletter, or social media. Some services allow the author to choose whether or not their review is public. If the review is less than satisfactory, the author can decline to make the review public.

Since the reviews tend to be so detailed, I'd recommend using the review in other areas on Amazon and beyond. The first place you should post the review is through Amazon Author Central. Simply locate your book, select editorial reviews, and post the review there.

Based on the service provider, Amazon Author Central may limit what you can share. Make sure you read the fine print in advance. For instance, Union Square Review did an editorial review of *Amazon Keywords for Books* (DaleLinks.com/UnionSquareReview). Their request was to share the link to the original review post. That was easy enough!

Though Union Square Review is new to editorial reviews, their reviewers are experienced professionals from all walks of the publishing business.

You may want to take advantage of the well-written editorial review and post it on your website. Just be sure to include a link to your book on Amazon for further context. Also, toss the editorial review in your book, on the cover, or in future editions. It wouldn't hurt to include the editorial review in a press kit when you're trying to land an interview or appearance. When you're reaching out to potential readers for reviews, you can use the editorial review for enticing them to read on. These types of reviews are great for third-party credibility, so take advantage of every opportunity to use it.

The biggest issue when it comes to editorial reviews is the cost. Editorial reviews are not cheap and can range anywhere from $249 to as much as $575. Be selective with who you choose. I included a list of reputable editorial review services in the back of the book. Get editorial reviews if you can afford to do so and have thick skin. Just take heed, an editorial review will not be the ultimate solution to your marketing and promotional needs. Getting the review will not be life-changing. In some instances, an editorial review can be defeating and leave you feeling a little beat up with a little less money. Proceed with caution and only invest in editorial reviews when you can afford it.

*I*n my book *Amazon Keywords for Books*, I touched on the value of getting reviews and building relevance for your title in the Amazon algorithm. Relevance is what Amazon deems as a product's ability to convert a browsing customer into a buyer. To further lend relevance to your book, you can post a comment on every review. This feature is nice and can be a way to build a sense of community around your book.

Be careful when responding to reviews. This road is fraught with dangers and big-time issues. Those who are thin-skinned will never make it to their next book if they aren't careful.

Should an author respond to reviews? Sure. I believe it does show you're actively welcoming feedback. When a reader sees the author took the time to respond to their review, then chances are likely, the reader will:

A. Respond and keep the conversation going

B. Read another book by the author

C. Share their experience about you with other people

After all, it's pretty cool when your favorite author takes the time to read your review, comment on it, and continue the dialogue. In the process, you're simply helping your book by building relevance with the search engine algorithm.

Let's be clear, though, not all reviews are going to be nice. You're not going to like what some people have to say, so how do you respond? Should you respond at all?

To me, it's an all or nothing approach. If you're going to take the time to bask in the glory of a 5-star review, then you need to also humble yourself in the dumpster fire of a 1-star troll. I'd recommend being selective with whether or not you will respond to a review.

If you are going to respond to a review, remember to keep it professional. You might be naturally inclined to pal around with a reader who gave you a great review. That's all well and good, but it tends to send mixed signals when that same reader comes back, dumping on you for a future book. While you stay professional for one, you need to be extra careful with the other. Low reviews are going to have you gritting your teeth and holding back a bit.

Remember, the reviewer did invest in your product, and they have every opportunity to ask for a refund from Amazon. With the liberal thirty-day return policy, a reviewer can and might return your book. Here's the scary thing, the review can remain after the refund.

When it comes to responding to reviews, you'll want to remember a few things:

1. Thank the reviewer first. Remember, they just spent time and money on your book. Those are two valuable commodities you should never take lightly.

2. Be empathetic regardless of the positive or negative tone. It's good to restate key points of feedback in the review.

3. Be brief and share any relevant insights where necessary.

4. Don't get defensive, and don't reject praise. Be grateful.

To further encourage a sense of community, share any interesting reviews with your current readership, social media following, or email list. You'll find it's a great way to prompt other people to leave a review for your book. It's also an indirect way of promoting your book without being overly salesy.

Sharing good reviews works well. If a visitor likes a review, they can click the **Helpful** button below the review. The more customers who click the button, the more the review gets served at the top. This can work for and against you.

If a bad review gets enough helpful votes, it'll be the first thing browsing customers see on a page. That can work against you.

Whatever you do, don't send traffic, and coerce them to hit the **Helpful** button. You can bring attention to the feature, but don't manipulate the results simply to drive up your favorite review. As an example, you could send out an email with this call-to-action:

> "This book is the best book that has ever been written! 5 stars!" Amazon Reviewer
>
> What do you think about that review? Would you agree with it? If someone hasn't read my book, do you think it would be helpful or not? Check out the full review at (insert the review link here)...

You'll notice I didn't guide my email subscriber into doing one action or the other. I simply shared the review, asked for insights, and directed my subscribers to check out the review for themselves on Amazon. Don't forget to insert the link to the review. Most people will not bother checking out a review if there isn't a link.

> Bonus Tip: Insert a screenshot of the review. It tends to help with finding the review once your follower visits the product review page.

Whoops, This Review Doesn't Belong Here

Yep, it happens. Some ding-dong posted a review for a completely different product altogether. We're not entirely sure how it got there, but it did happen.

Then, some reviewers post a review despite never reading or buying the product. They'll even fully disclose they never purchased or read the book.

The last types of reviews are predatory or targeted harassment. Sadly, these types of reviews are nearly impossible to remove. You have to prove the reader is maliciously posting reviews on your products to drive away buyers or slow down sales. I tried disputing several predatory reviewers, but Amazon wouldn't hear of it. They feel it's important to allow all reviewers to post both positive and negative feedback. Anything short of a signed confession will not work to take the review down. Simply take it on the chin and move along.

If you begin to see a pattern of abuse, you can always contact Amazon and highlight the issues. However, don't hold your breath on the problem getting resolved. You can at least breathe a sigh of relief in knowing bad actors eventually hang themselves with their own rope. I found many predatory reviews eventually disappear along with the Amazon reviewer profile. When Amazon detects suspicious activity, they'll put that fire out in due time, especially with consistent and clear abuse of their community guidelines.

Also of note, Amazon is now allowing review ratings without representation. Essentially, readers can leave a star rating and do not have to justify it. This new feature can be good, but it can also be confusing for authors. Without knowing why someone rated a book a certain way, it's hard to adjust the publication. Of course, it's impossible to remove review ratings since no one knows who rated it and why.

Can You Share Amazon Reviews Elsewhere?

Amazon is protective of its trademark and property. Part of their property includes the reviews posted on their platform. Sadly, no clear guideline or rule states whether or not you can share their property on other sites. To err on the side of caution, share short snippets for reviews from Amazon when you do. It can fall under fair use, and you are somewhat safe.

> Fair use is a doctrine in the United States law permitting limited use of copyrighted content without having permission from the copyright holder.[23]

Be careful, though. Fair use isn't something you can abuse or have to protect you if you draw Amazon's ire. In my experience, I never heard of Amazon sending a DMCA takedown notice for sharing their reviews on a website, social media, through an email, or anywhere else.

I used to encourage authors to post a review through Amazon Author Central in the editorial reviews section. However, this creates redundancy on your product page and doesn't do anything but create more stuff for browsing customers to read. If you don't have an editorial review or reviews posted from other areas to share in the editorial reviews section, leave it blank.

O n Amazon, you have the hidden option to make an ebook permanently free. Even though Kindle Direct Publishing (KDP) will not allow you to price an ebook below ninety-nine cents, you can price it as free with a few extra steps. Publish your ebook through Kindle Direct Publishing but avoid opting into the KDP Select program. Then, publish your title on other sites like Apple, Barnes & Noble, Kobo, or Google Play Books where you can publish your title for free.

Once your title is available through the other sites, contact KDP through your dashboard and request a price match for your title. For a deeper dive into how and why you should publish a permafree book, be sure to check out my short guide, *Secrets of the Permafree Book* (DaleLinks.com/PermafreeBook).

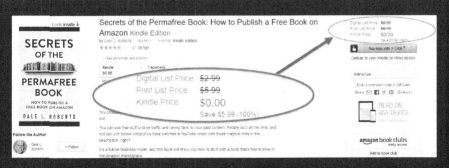

Even **Secrets of the Permafree Book** is set as permanently free in this example. It's a great way to garner more reviews and build brand awareness.

Once you make your title free, promote it just like you would any other book. You'll be amazed at how many more reviews you'll get organically. Why? It's free!

In 2015, my mentor challenged me to produce eight to ten short books for my fitness niche. He wanted me to publish the ebooks as permafree. It just so happened I was sitting on a few short reads already, so it wasn't a tall task. Once I published the books, I saw a huge increase in sales for my normally priced books. Also, there was an additional uptick in organic reviews, especially on the permafree books.

Fast forward to about 2018, and those same permafree books had a decent amount of reviews. Sadly, I didn't see as many downloads, and not as many buyers were going to the full-priced books. I switched the permafree books into fully paid books. The nice part was I didn't have to do any review gathering. People naturally left reviews over the three years since I published them.

Before you dive into this methodology, you need to be aware it comes with its share of heartaches. When you allow readers to download your ebooks for free, quite a few people will do so and feel entitled to beat up the publication. I discussed this issue with several other authors in other niches. They expressed the same. Whenever a book is free, a different subset of hyper-critical readers grab a copy and leave a bad review. It's not to say the free book readers ruined my book with bad reviews, but you certainly see lower reviews across the board.

This may have a lot to do with the perceived value. If a customer sees an item is free, they'll value it far less than a full-priced book. We could even theorize those lacking the funds typically have a different mindset than those who can afford full-priced books. So, their expectations are going to be a bit more grandiose.

Nonetheless, if you want to get more organic reviews, one of the easiest ways is to make your ebook free. Then, promote the heck out of the book to get more downloads. Once you get so many downloads, you can expect to see more organic reviews.

One of the biggest missed opportunities right now in self-publishing is in audiobooks. If you do not have your work published in audiobooks, then you must not skip this chapter. You'll discover why getting reviews through audiobooks is even easier than print and ebook. To make matters better, Amazon equips you with all you need to get more reviews on your books.

When you publish your audiobook exclusively through the Amazon-owned Audiobook Creation Exchange (ACX), you get up to 100 promotional codes per audiobook. These codes are a great way to gift copies for the audiobook marketplace, Audible. In turn, your readers – or in this case, listeners – will hopefully leave a review.

In years past, ACX had a glaring hole in their system where promotional codes were good for any audiobook on Audible. In early 2020, ACX closed up the loophole. Now, promotional codes are only good for a given audiobook while carrying no monetary value.

Think of the Audible promo codes as a way to build an ARC team for your audiobooks. Sadly, since ACX doesn't have a pre-order feature at this time, it's technically not an advanced copy. That's okay because the result is the same.

Follow the same best practices when it comes to soliciting reviews. You can reach out to your current readership, influencers, bloggers,

YouTubers, and beyond. Nothing is off-limits when it comes to getting reviews on the Audible platform, and that's where the issue lies.

The listeners will download and listen to your audiobook. Then, they can leave a review on Audible, not Amazon. Can the listener leave an unverified purchase review on Amazon? Sure! You can even recommend it once they've posted a review on Audible. For now, there's no integration between Audible to Amazon with the reviews. It's the opposite for the other way around.

On Audible, browsing customers can see the reviews posted on Amazon for the book under a special tab next to the Audible Reviews. Having the Amazon reviews integrated on Audible is a plus. It would just be nice to see it reciprocated on the Amazon platform for Audible reviews. Then, product listings would get even more reviews to build social proof.

I believe Amazon and Audible will eventually integrate both ways. Not too long ago, Amazon allowed for cross-region propagation of reviews. Previously, you could only see U.S. reviews in the U.S. and U.K. reviews in the U.K. Now, see all the reviews across every region on most Amazon sites. Amazon does take a while to post the reviews across all sites, but they are showing up eventually.

Since Amazon is always changing, tweaking, and evolving their website for a better customer experience, I imagine we'll see an Audible and Amazon integration. You can then see more than just two product review types – in ebook, print books, and audiobooks.

Other Audiobook Promo Codes

Another platform to publish your audiobook is Findaway Voices. This audiobook publishing platform distributes to over forty different audiobook retail sites and libraries. When you publish through Findaway Voices, you get thirty promotional codes good for the Author's Direct audiobook platform. If you publish exclusively through Findaway Voices, then you get 100 promotional codes.

The idea works the same way as Audible promo codes do. You send the promo code, and the listener gets a free download of your audiobook. The listener can then leave a review on their preferred audiobook platform. In theory, your listener could post an unverified purchase review of your audiobook on Amazon.

If you want wider distribution beyond what ACX offers, then you may want to consider Findaway Voices. The only catch is you must agree to be non-exclusive on ACX. You then get smaller royalties (25% non-exclusive versus 40% exclusive). Findaway Voices realized the predicament of losing the Audible promotional codes and, in turn, made up for it through their promo code system.

Audiobook Promo Code Sites & Facebook Groups

Much like getting reviews for your print books and ebooks, you can get readers through various websites and services. Focus on the author and reader websites first. Some services will cost you. For instance, AudiobookBoom.com has a premium service where you can advertise your audiobook promotional codes through their email newsletter or website. When listeners are interested in getting a promo code, Audiobook Boom will send you an email notification with all the pertinent contact information.

One of the best resources yet is Facebook Groups. Simply visit Facebook, search "audiobook promo codes" or "free audiobooks," and you'll get many groups devoted to connecting listeners with authors. This is, by far, the best free resource for getting reviews.

The one advantage audiobooks have over print and ebooks is accessibility. It's much easier to listen to an audiobook than to sit down and read it yourself. You can listen to an audiobook in almost any situation and adjust the reading speed to blaze through the content quicker. Once you publish an audiobook, I highly recommend getting those promotional codes out to as many listeners as possible who are willing to post a review after listening.

I had a book once that got a one-star review right after publishing. The low review crushed me! The reviewer clearly had a bias against the topic. In no way was he willing to read or learn more about the content. They planned to push their opposing viewpoint. In a panic, I tried my best to get reviews. Since the topic was a rather niche subject, finding reviewers wasn't going to be easy.

Despite the low review, the sales kept coming in. After a while, I abandoned the search for more reviews while focusing on higher priorities. While I managed other tasks, I had Amazon ads sending traffic to the one-star rated book. Oddly enough, customers still bought the book. Slowly, more positive reviews rolled in and buried the negative review. During the time between, the book continued to get consistent sales.

Can reviews really make or break the success of a book? Well, this depends largely on what you do with them. I mentioned how you could reframe negative reviews in a way that draws in more positive reviews. I even shared how you can share positive reviews to get more engagement on your product page. I explained how commenting helps build a sense of community around your book.

Suppose you simply roll over and expect Amazon to dish out buying customers who'll also post a review. In that case, you're going to be in for a rude awakening. You must put in the effort to see some type of return. Having a book published on Amazon isn't enough to get sales or gather reviews. You need to have a consistent action plan that includes gathering reviews for your books.

Will you always get reviews from every reader? No, but you greatly increase your odds of winning if you play the game. You cannot play the game with your hands in your pockets or through inconsistent practices. Know where you're going, how you're getting there, and what you need to do to improve your results.

Also, it's not good enough for you to simply gather reviews and call it a day. You need to read the reviews and take notes. Your readers tell you what they like best about your book and what needs to change about it. Before you do make any changes, it's a good idea to take it all with a grain of salt.

One adage holds true when it comes to reviews:

> If one person calls you an ass, ignore them. If five people call you an ass, buy a saddle.

One review might not be enough to draw a conclusion. You may need numerous reviews saying the same thing before you consider adjusting your publication. How many reviews are enough to draw statistical significance? That's going to be up to you.

My book, *The Home Workout Plan for Seniors,* is a prime example of an egregious oversight on my part. In concept, the content made sense, but in practice, I failed. When I launched the book, I had a handful of happy reviews. Then, I noticed a few trickling in from the U.K. They were not happy with the content and for a good reason.

My big oversight was in how I formatted the content for the audience. Since senior citizens would read the content, it would've been in my best interests to make the print large and the pictures even larger still. Sadly, I formatted the content like any other book, and I paid dearly in the reviews.

For whatever reason, life called me away from my fitness books, and I never found the time to update the content. When I finally did get around to fixing the interior, the reviews were brutal. A majority of the reviews complained about the small print and smaller pictures. They had every right to complain, and I had to take it on the chin. Rather than roll over, I course-corrected, updated the content, and kept the low reviews.

Quite a few readers were unhappy, and I listened to their requests. Now, the book continues to sell a few copies here and there. Will it ever recover from the pounding it took from the reviews? Time will tell. Maybe I need to take a bit of my own advice and slap a few more reviews on the book now that it's updated.

Getting reviews isn't difficult, but it isn't so easy you can sit back and just have them rain down from nowhere. While selling books alone is difficult, you can certainly lighten the burden by getting a bit of social proof through reviews. Can reviews make or break the success of your book? That's entirely up to what you do about it. What will *you* do?

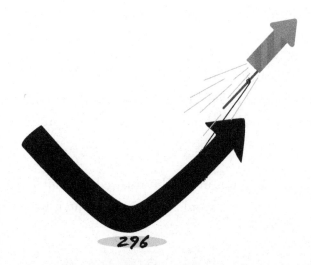

*A*fter the first time I visited Condado Tacos, I waddled out of the restaurant and immediately fumbled for my phone. My first inclination was to leave a detailed review because I didn't want anyone else to miss out on the same experience I enjoyed. It would also commemorate the great time I had throwing down more tacos than my stomach should ever handle at any one time. Indirectly, I helped build just a little credibility for this small restaurant tucked below a luxury apartment building in the heart of downtown Columbus.

Could Condado Tacos exist or even thrive without my review or the countless others left online? Sure, but it'd be that much harder to drive traffic into their establishment. They most likely would have to spend a ton of money on marketing and promotion through mail-out ads or commercials on the radio. Why waste money on it? Customer reviews are the best type of advertising, and they're free!

If you're ever at an impasse, and you're wondering if anyone will ever buy your book, you need to take a hard look at your review gathering process. Once you start getting reviews, it's important to keep the traffic coming to your book and build awareness about the value of leaving a review of your book. Also, never stop asking for reviews. When you do get reviews, show enough self-awareness to adjust your book to suit the readers. That way, you aren't blindly pushing forward to the detriment of your book. As some people say, "Don't cut off your nose to spite your face."

Much like Condado Tacos or any other company, service, or product, it's going to take time to build trust in the public eye. Focus on your long game. It's going to be awhile to amass enough social proof to gain random strangers' trust. That's what getting reviews is all about – getting enough validation from an outside party that merits other people trying you out too.

When you get beat up by a low-star review or some disparaging words, remember even the best books, brands, and companies have dealt with it before. Once you've hit that point, remind yourself you've made it! Everyone from JK Rowling to Charles Dickens to Stephen King to Tony Robbins has low reviews. Never throw the towel in if you get beat up a little in the reviews.

As we wrap up this book about getting reviews, I want to leave you with a final thought. Getting reviews is an integral part of any marketing and promotional plan. Marketing and promotion are a never-ending task. It's not like you can publish your book on Amazon, run a few ad campaigns, and then call it a day. Suppose you want long term, sustainable earnings from your books. In that case, you'll have to devote most of your energy and resources to marketing and promotion. Part of that promotional strategy should be getting reviews. As you discovered from this book, it doesn't have to cost a dime most of the time. When it does, you need to measure the effectiveness before ever trying it again.

One last thing before you go out there and get your book reviews—it's not enough you learn the best practices for getting book reviews. You must implement the knowledge. Simply reading a book about getting reviews is not going to give you reviews alone. Much like getting a gym membership, you actually have to do the work to reap the results. Once you do kick into action and start getting reviews, reward yourself with a tasty taco. You deserve it!

Self Publisher ▾ **A Small Ask...**

Now that you finished reading this book, what did you think of what you read? Were there any tips or information you found insightful? What do you think was missing from this book? While you're thinking back on what you read, it'd mean the world to me if you left an honest review on Amazon.

As you know, reviews play an integral part in building relevancy for all products. So whether you found the information helpful or not, your candid review would help other customers make an informed purchase.

Also, based on your review, I'll adjust this publication and future editions. That way, you and other indie authors can learn and grow.

Feel free to leave a review at DaleLinks.com/AmazonBook.

Dale L. Roberts is a self-publishing advocate, award-winning author, and video content creator. Dale's inherent passion for life fuels his self-publishing advocacy both in print and online. After publishing over 40 titles and becoming an international bestselling author on Amazon, Dale started his YouTube channel, *Self-Publishing with Dale.* Voted by Feedspot among the Top 50 YouTube channels about self-publishing, Dale cemented his position as the indie-author community's go-to authority.

Dale currently lives with his wife Kelli and cat Izzie in Columbus, Ohio.

Relevant links:

- Website – SelfPublishingWithDale.com

- YouTube – YouTube.com/SelfPublishingWithDale

- Twitter – Twitter.com/SelfPubWithDale

- Facebook – Facebook.com/SelfPubWithDale

- Instagram – Instagram.com/SelfPubWithDale

- DON'T GO HERE! – DaleLinks.com

Get More Book Sales Today!

You wrote the book.

And now it's published.

But you're not getting any sales! What gives?!

Most people would have you believe self-publishing on Amazon is easy. Yet why aren't you seeing the results they claim you should get?

Your lack of book sales comes down to 3 culprits:

- Keywords

- Marketing and promotion

- Book reviews

It's time you put all your self-publishing woes to bed and finally increase your book sales for good.

Enter The Amazon Self-Publisher series.

You'll learn:

- The secrets to keyword research and selection

- Cheap yet effective book promotions

- How to get book reviews the legit way

- Where Amazon Advertising will serve your book best

And hundreds of powerful insights!

You'll love learning all about Amazon self-publishing, because once you discover proven strategies in self-publishing, your life will change for the good.

Order this 3-part series now when you visit…

DaleLinks.com/ASP

Self Publisher ▼	Special Thanks	Q

*f*irst and foremost, I big thank you goes out to every single reader and members on the advanced reader copy team. It means the world to me that you spent your time, energy, attention, and in most cases, money, on my little books devoted to Amazon self-publishing. Without your support and encouragement, this entire series would never have a chance. Because of you, I'm able to write about what I love. I hope in return you gain a little more insight into this crazy little business and grow your own author brand in the process.

Rather than copy and paste previous special thanks, I'm going to break it off into sections of people who directly influence me or have some hand in my development.

To my family and closest friends – my wife Kelli, Walt, Russ Webster, Harold Webb, my mother Kaye Cox, Vicki Hass, Kari and Julian, Kenzie and Anthony, Patty and David, my dad Mike Roberts and Nancy, Uncle Mike Johnson, and Colleen Schlea.

To my self-publishing family – Ava Fails, Rob Archangel, Julie Broad, Dave Chesson, Keith Wheeler, Kevin Maguire, Mojo Siedlak, Michael La Ronn, Catrina "TheLadyWrites" Taylor, Mark Brownless, Scott Jay Marshall II, Andrew Wong, Jonel Fernando, JanMarie Kelly, Hannah & Jay Jacobson, John "My Writing Partner in Crime" Fitch, John Waaser, Jacob Rothenberg, Su Singh, Chandler Bolt, Jason Jones, Willie Mays, Omanah Bultman, Brittany Putzer, Lafiro

303

Gomez III, Kyle Atkinson, Bonnie Phillips, Sylvia Hubbard, Lee Jones, Saketh Kumar, Orna Ross and the entire ALLi team, Walter Weyburn, and so many more.

To my video creator family – Dan Norton, Dan Currier, Jason Stallworth, Nick Nimmin, Brian G Johnson, Andrew Kan, Eddie Garrison, Doug Hewson, Regor Onafetsid, Derral Eves, Jeremy Vest, Roberto Blake, the entire TubeBuddy team, Rob Balasabas, Shannon Vlogs, Evan and Nina Carmichael, Helen Kinson, Christina Sisson, Terrance at Inside the Lab PC Tech, Owen Video, Nico from Morningfame, Marcus Campbell, Jeff Eatley, Gord Isman, Andru Edwards, Ryan A Raymond, and so many more. I can't begin to recall them all.

To the brands and companies who believed in me – BookDoggy, Fiverr, Findaway Voices, ProWritingAid, Thinkific, Vexels, Romance Publishing Academy, Kotobee Author, Lulu, IntoTheAM, Restream, Streamlabs, and Winning Writers. And the others who had my back including Draft2Digital, Kobo, IngramSpark, and I'm sure I forgot someone. Sorry.

Self Publisher ▼ | **Amazon Keywords for Books Resources**

The 5 Best Kindlepreneur Articles

1. Kindlepreneur Book Description Generator:
   https://dalelinks.com/html2

2. Keywords in the Book Description:
   https://kindlepreneur.com/keywords-in-your-book-description/

3. Sell More Books with Amazon Book Ads:
   https://dalelinks.com/amscourse

4. The Secret Method to Choosing Amazon Book Categories:
   https://dalelinks.com/choosecategories

5. +127 of the Top Free and Paid Book Promotion Sites:
   https://kindlepreneur.com/list-sites-promote-free-amazon-books/

The 5 Must-Read Books on Self-Publishing

1. *Mastering Amazon Ads & Mastering Amazon Descriptions* by Brian Meeks

2. *How to Write a Sizzling Synopsis* by Bryan Cohen

3. *Become a Successful Indie Author* by Craig Martelle

4. *Self-Publisher's Legal Handbook* by Helen Sedwick

5. *Successful Self-Publishing* by Joanna Penn

The 5 Must-Watch YouTube Channels Devoted to Self-Publishing

1. Book Launchers:
   https://www.youtube.com/user/julieabroad

2. Keith Wheeler Books:
   https://www.youtube.com/channel/UCcFfP0Px7cO3h6BCZUpXUQQ

3. Kindlepreneur:
   https://www.youtube.com/channel/UC-s3Pb8uIBm0QN8MVaulJKA

4. Draft2Digital:
   https://www.youtube.com/channel/UCCxkNFCpyAoQV5eAKbZwZHg

5. Author Level Up:
   https://www.youtube.com/channel/UCcdjxp-TGOOucIV1rMDS8jw

Self Publisher ▼ **Promotional Strategies for Books Resources**

- Archangel Ink -- DaleLinks.com/ArchangelInk
- Advanced Reader Copy hosting
  - Storyorigin – StoryOrig.in
  - Fiveabook – Fiveabook.com
  - NOTE: Both websites are in open beta and may switch to a premium model at any time. Get access while they're still free!
- Background removal by Fiverr – DaleLinks.com/Kaysar
- Book Brush – for free and premium graphic assets – think Canva for authors on steroids –BookBrush.com.
- Books about Amazon Ads
  - Brian Meeks – *Mastering Amazon Ads*
  - Chris Fox – *Ads for Authors Who Don't Like Math*
- Books about email marketing
  - *Invisible Selling Machine* by Ryan Deiss
  - *Dotcom Secrets* by Russel Brunson
- Captioning services by Rev – DaleLinks.com/Rev.
- Free image resources:
  - Pixabay - Pixabay.com
  - Vecteezy - Vecteezy.com
  - Pexels - Pexels.com/

- > Visual Hunt - Visualhunt.com/
- > Unsplash - Unsplash.com/
- > Gratisography - Gratisography.com
- > Freepik - Freepik.com
- > New Old Stock - Nos.twnsnd.co
- > Stock Snap - Stocksnap.io
- > Flickr - Flickr.com/creativecommons
- > Free Images - Freeimages.com
- > Wikimedia - Commons.wikimedia.org/wiki/Main_Page
- Image background removal – Remove.bg at DaleLinks.com/RemoveBG
- Jason Jones publicist – DaleLinks.com/PRToolkit
- Publisher Rocket – DaleLinks.com/Rocket
- Social media automation by ContentStudio – DaleLinks.com/ContentStudio
- YouTube experts I trust & follow
  - > Nick Nimmin - YouTube.com/NickNimmin
  - > Brian G Johnson - YouTube.com/BrianGJohnsonTV
    - * Tube Ritual on FB - Facebook.com/groups/TubeRitual
  - > Roberto Blake - YouTube.com/RobertoBlakePSD
  - > Derral Eves - YouTube.com/DerralEves

- The Alliance of Independent Authors (ALLi) Watchdog Services - https://selfpublishingadvice.org/best-self-publishing-services/
- Hidden Gems Books The Good and Bad of Amazon's $50 Review Rule - https://www.hiddengemsbooks.com/amazons-50-review-rule/
- Kindlepreneur: HOW TO GET FREE BOOK REVIEWS WITH NO BLOG, NO LIST, AND NO BEGGING - https://kindlepreneur.com/how-to-get-book-reviews-with-no-blog-no-list-and-no-begging/
- Reedsy
  - › Best Book Review Blogs of 2020 - https://blog.reedsy.com/book-review-blogs/
  - › The Best Book Review Sites For Enthusiastic Readers - https://reedsy.com/discovery/blog/book-review-sites
  - › Reedsy Discovery - https://reedsy.com/discovery/submit

Review Sites & Services

- Book Blogger List - https://bookbloggerlist.com/
- Book Reviewer Yellow Pages - https://bookrevieweryellowpages.com/book-bloggers/
- Digital Pubbing - https://digitalpubbing.com/7-strategies-and-94-tools-to-help-indie-authors-find-readers-and-reviewers/
- Kate McKillan's Outbox Online Design Studio - https://www.outboxonline.com/book-review-submission/

- Library Journal - https://www.libraryjournal.com/?page=Review-Submissions
- Library Thing - https://www.librarything.com/
- Self-Publishing Review - https://www.selfpublishingreview.com/spr-bestseller-book-packages/
- The Indie View - http://www.theindieview.com/indie-reviewers/
- Triskele Books - http://triskelebooks.blogspot.com/2013/03/indie-friendly-book-reviewers.html
- Tweet Your Books - https://www.tweetyourbooks.com/p/free-reviews.html
- Writing World - https://www.tweetyourbooks.com/p/free-reviews.html

Editorial Reviews

- Foreword Reviews - https://publishers.forewordreviews.com/reviews/
- Clarion Reviews - https://publishers.forewordreviews.com/reviews/#service-clarion-review
- Kirkus Reviews - https://www.kirkusreviews.com/indie-reviews/
- Union Square Reviews - https://unionsquarereview.com/
- Independent Book Review - https://www.selfpublishingreview.com/spr-bestseller-book-packages/
- NetGalley - https://www.netgalley.com/

Audiobook Promo Code Sites

- Audiobook Boom – https://audiobookboom.com/authors
- Audiofreebies - https://www.audiofreebies.com/add-an-audiobook/
- Audiobooks Unleashed - https://audiobooksunleashed.com/add-an-audiobook/
- Free Audiobook Codes - https://freeaudiobookcodes.com/advertisers/

1   Chesson, Dave. (n.d.) KINDLE KEYWORD RANKING PERCENTAGES: #1 VS. #2. Kindlepreneur.com. https://kindlepreneur.com/kindle-keyword-ranking-percentages-1-vs-2/

2   Chesson, Dave. (May 29, 2020) KEYWORDS IN YOUR BOOK DESCRIPTION: DO THEY HELP? Kindlepreneur.com. https://kindlepreneur.com/keywords-in-your-book-description/

3   Book Industry Study Group. (n.d.) BISAC Subject Codes FAQ. Book Industry Standard Group. https://bisg.org/page/BISACFaQ

4   Kindle Direct Publishing. (n.d.) Make Your Book More Discoverable with Keywords. Kindle Direct Publishing. https://kdp.amazon.com/en_US/help/topic/G201298500

5   Chesson, Dave. (n.d.) 7 KINDLE KEYWORDS: USE ALL 50 CHARACTERS OR NOT? Kindlepreneur.com https://kindlepreneur.com/7-kindle-keywords/

6   Amazon.com, Inc. (n.d.) FAQ. Advertising.amazon.com. https://advertising.amazon.com/resources/faq

7   Amazon.com, Inc. (n.d.) Help.Adveritising.amazon.com. https://advertising.amazon.com/help?entityId=ENTITY2358XJVOPHN6

8   Google Ads Help. (n.d.) Quality Score: Definition. Google Ads. https://support.google.com/google-ads/answer/140351

9   Martelle, Craig. (March 26, 2018) Become a Successful Indie Author: Work Toward Your Writing Dream. Page 22.

10   Clement, J. (10 August 2020). Number of monthly active Facebook users worldwide as of 2nd quarter 2020. https://www.statista.com/statistics/264810/number-of-monthly-active-facebook-users-worldwide/.

11   IEEE Communications Society. (10 June 2017). Cisco: Online video to account for 82% of all Internet traffic by 2021! https://techblog.comsoc.org/2017/06/10/cisco-increased-use-of-web-video-to-be-82-of-all-internet-traffic-by-2021/.

12   Hubspot, Inc. (25 September 2018). The Top 7 Search Engines, Ranked by Popularity. https://blog.hubspot.com/marketing/top-search-engines.

13   D'Anastasio, C. (22 June 2020). Microsoft Gives Up on Mixer. https://www.wired.com/story/microsoft-shutting-down-mixer-facebook-gaming/.

14   Kim, E. (25 August 2014). Amazon Buys Twitch For $970 Million In Cash. https://www.businessinsider.com/amazon-buys-twitch-2014-8.

15   Schultz, M. (n.d.). How Many Touches Does It Take to Make a Sale? https://www.rainsalestraining.com/blog/how-many-touches-does-it-take-to-make-a-sale.

16   Collinger, T. (n.d.) How Online Reviews Influence Sales. https://spiegel.medill.northwestern.edu/online-reviews/.

17   Amazon.com LLC. (n.d.) Community Guidelines. https://www.amazon.com/gp/help/customer/display.html.

18   Amazon.com LLC. (n.d.) About Amazon Verified Purchase Reviews. https://www.amazon.com/gp/help/customer/display.html?nodeId=202076110.

19   Cooper. D. (24 July 2015). Amazon accused of spying on reviewer's social media profiles. https://www.engadget.com/2015-07-24-amazon-social-media-ebook-review-relationship-imy-santiago.html.

20   Chesson, D. (8 February 2019) THE ULTIMATE GUIDE TO GOODREADS FOR AUTHORS. https://kindlepreneur.com/how-to-use-goodreads-for-authors/#anchor-2.

21   Gaughran, D. (2 June 2018) When #Cockygate And #Tiffanygate Collide. https://davidgaughran.com/2018/06/02/cockygate-faleena-hopkins-tiffanygate-chance-carter/.

22   Rutkowska, A. (n.d.) BOOK LAUNCH REVIEWS: LAUNCHING WITH 100+ REVIEWS. https://kindlepreneur.com/book-launch-reviews-launching-with-100-reviews/

23   Library of Congress. (n.d.) More Information on Fair Use. https://copyright.gov/fair-use/more-info.html.

Made in the USA
Coppell, TX
23 October 2022

85148453R00177